JANE AUSTEN'S NOTEBOOK

The Life, Times and Writings of

Jane Austen

Written and Compiled by
SOPHIE COLLINS

The History Press

© 2025 Quarto Publishing plc

First published in the United Kingdom in 2025 by
The History Press
97 St. George's Place
Cheltenham
Gloucestershire
GL50 3QB
www.thehistorypress.co.uk

Printed in China

This book may not be reproduced in whole or in part, in any form or by any means, electronic or mechanical, including photocopying, recording, or by any information storage and retrieval system now known or hereafter invented, without written permission from the publisher.

2 4 6 8 10 9 7 5 3 1

ISBN: 978-1-80399-893-0

Conceived, designed and produced by
The Bright Press, an imprint of The Quarto Group
1 Triptych Place, London, SE1 9SH, United Kingdom.
T (0)20 7700 6700
www.quarto.com

Design by: Lindsey Johns

Contents

INTRODUCTION
6

CHAPTER ONE
A CLERGYMAN'S DAUGHTER
9

CHAPTER TWO
BECOMING A WRITER
33

CHAPTER THREE
ADULTHOOD
57

CHAPTER FOUR
CHAWTON
83

CHAPTER FIVE
ADVENTURES IN PUBLISHING
107

CHAPTER SIX
ILLNESS, DEATH AND LEGACY
133

BIBLIOGRAPHY AND REFERENCES 156
INDEX 158
CREDITS 160

Introduction

FINDING JANE

For a modern reader, trying to find the 'real' Jane Austen can feel like an archaeological dig. The top layer mostly consists of familiar images from film and TV adaptations – you might uncover an arch Anya Taylor-Joy or a dripping Colin Firth – before you go down a bit further to find the revered subject of 20th-century critics. On the next layer, there's the Victorian version, the writer of heartwarming drawing-room romances, that can be read and reread without finding anything disruptive. Deeper layers offer a bit more of the Georgian Austen – unsentimental, and often hard-headed. But if you're looking for the person, rather than the author, she remains shadowy.

Her potted biography is straightforward: the seventh of eight children of a vicar, who grew up in rural Hampshire in the last quarter of the 18th century. She served her dues as a useful member of a large family, and she remained single, which would have meant that she became poorer and of less consequence socially as she grew old. She didn't get the chance, though, dying at just 41, when her name hadn't yet appeared on any of her published books. The simplicity of her life, which was overstressed by the first genteel memoir, written by her nephew, made her achievements seem incredible.

Her large and lively set of siblings, though, gave her a much wider perspective, and she took full advantage of it. James, the eldest, was a country vicar, like her father, but through Edward she saw what it was to be rich, while Henry Austen – a sharp operator in today's terms – played the modest hand he was dealt to best advantage, weaving his way through

a variety of careers from army officer to banker. Frank and Charles, the naval brothers, gave her insights into an active life at sea. The Austens were a tight clan, and their only two sisters, Jane and Cassandra, were conversant with all the details of their lives. Jane had her material; she could draw from all of them, knowing, as most of her contemporaries did not, that it was sensible to write about what was familiar.

An Unmistakeable Voice

We finally find her personal voice in her letters. They're funny, clear-sighted, opinionated – and include some startlingly caustic, even heartless, asides. The sweet, observant spinster revered by the Victorians would never have laughed over her neighbour's stillbirth, as Austen did, nor written such excoriating descriptions of her fellow guests at a ball, with their fat necks, pink husbands and diamond bandeaux. Ouch.

That her stories were different can be spotted very early, long before the first letter we have, in her juvenile works – it's there in the surreal freedom with which her heroines run amok, and her characters glide in and out of wildly constructed plots. And although the acerbic tone becomes measured with the mature novels, her sense of the ridiculous develops to a fine point; she takes characterisation to a new level, and introduces the use of multiple viewpoints, too. Later commentators – Charlotte Brontë, for instance – inclined to sneer at the confined settings of Jane's 'ladies and gentlemen' and seemingly had no idea of what they owed to Austen as a pioneer.

The books were slow burners rather than instant hits, waxing and waning in popularity for decades after her death, and she wasn't acknowledged as one of the great English novelists until the 20th century. As Virginia Woolf found, she's hard to catch in the act of greatness, but we know it when we see it. To make her out more clearly, we need to start at the beginning, with the vicar's younger daughter, born into an unusually energetic and literary family, and watch as she grows.

Above left: Although Austen's plots tend to be girl-heavy – here, the five Bennet sisters are suffering a reading by Mr Collins – Austen's own childhood was populated by boys: five of her brothers and the boarders at her parents' small school.

Above: A drawing taken from a much-disputed portrait that is sometimes claimed to be Jane in childhood. Apart from her disabled brother George, she was the only Austen sibling who never had a portrait taken professionally – even Cassandra survives in a late silhouette.

Opposite page: The Austen we know, at several removes from the original. First repainted – posthumously – from a rough sketch by Cassandra, then engraved from the painting, and subsequently reproduced whenever her portrait was needed, although none of her family thought it looked like her.

CHAPTER ONE

A Clergyman's Daughter

The Reverend George Austen

A CLERGYMAN'S LIVING
A country vicar's income might come from the profits of glebe lands – which were farmed directly for the benefit of the parish clergyman – or, if the parish's farming lands had been privately sold, from a tithe of 10 per cent of farming profits, paid directly by parishioners. It was not unusual for a clergyman to have more than one parish, as George Austen did.

Austen's father was born in Kent, in 1731, the son of William, a surgeon, and his wife Rebecca, who died giving birth to George's younger sister when he was still an infant. A few years later, William Austen remarried then died – in rapid succession – whereupon his widow cast out her stepchildren, the newly orphaned George and his two sisters, pushing them into a dependence on their father's extended family.

Family Support

Luckily there were plenty of aunts and uncles for the three to fall back on. George and his sisters, Philadelphia and Leonora, went first to neglectful Uncle Stephen, a London bookseller; George was then settled on an aunt in Kent, where he attended Tonbridge School. Fortunately another uncle, Francis Austen, an attorney who, by working hard and marrying well, had amassed a considerable fortune, took an interest in his nephew and nieces. His patronage and contacts helped to give George a start. From school, he was awarded a place at St John's College, Oxford, where he studied divinity and was first appointed assistant chaplain and subsequently proctor, a senior college management post.

Not only was he quick and clever, George was good-looking too, with hazel eyes, thick hair and a straight nose. Those looks, which led him to be known as 'the handsome proctor' in Oxford, must have played a part in his appeal to his future wife, Cassandra Leigh, who was staying with her uncle Theophilus Leigh, then Master of Balliol, when the couple first met. Particularly his nose: she was known to be fussy about noses.

'I have always understood that he was considered extremely handsome, and it was a beauty which stood by him all his life... His eyes were not large, but of a peculiar and bright hazel. My aunt Jane's were something like them...'

—Anna Lefroy, Jane's niece, remembering George Austen's good looks

His marriage meant that he had to leave his job at Oxford, which was open to single men only. Luckily his relatives came to the rescue again. Useful Uncle Francis proposed George for the parish of Deane, in Hampshire, while the Knights, a rich family who were George's fourth cousins, gifted him a second living in the parish of nearby Steventon. Between them, the parishes raised just enough income for him to provide for a wife and family.

His tough start no doubt helped to shape George Austen's character – he was kindly, practical and engaged with all his children, but he didn't tolerate slackers or moaners. Effort and hard work were warmly applauded, and he followed their lives closely, offering sensible and often amusing advice.

Above: A portrait of a rather severe-looking George Austen in middle age.

Opposite page: St John's College, Oxford, where George became a Fellow – as would two of his sons, James and Henry.

The First Cassandra

MISSING MOTHERS
Cassandra's children seem to have been dutiful towards her, especially after their father's death, but there is no evidence that Jane was close to her mother, and one looks in vain for a likely portrait of her in the novels: Mrs Bennet (*Pride and Prejudice*) thinks only of getting her daughters advantageously married, while Lady Bertram (*Mansfield Park*) is an indulged and lazy fool. In the same novel, Fanny Price, Austen's mousiest heroine, has an absent mother with whom she cannot bond when she finally re-meets her in adulthood. Emma Woodhouse (*Emma*) and Anne Elliot (*Persuasion*) are both motherless, while Mrs Dashwood (*Sense and Sensibility*) is rather too full of sentiment to be a sensible advocate. Perhaps there's a faint echo of something familiar in the mother of Catherine Morland (*Northanger Abbey*) – who is over-busy but still practical, with 'useful plain sense'.

Most readers today make an immediate link with Austen's sister when they hear the name, but the first Cassandra in Jane's life was her mother, Cassandra Leigh. Born in 1739, she too was the daughter of a clergyman and although not rich came from less precarious circumstances than those of her future husband: the Leighs were old Warwickshire gentry and had a broad network of useful connections, including both aristocrats and intellectuals in their family tree.

A Happy Marriage

Dark-haired, with grey eyes, Cassandra was handsome, clever and strong-minded; a silhouette made of her in old age (reproduced below) shows a firm profile with a prominent Roman nose – the 'family' nose, of which she was famously proud. She was cultured and enjoyed writing both poetry and prose.

Like her husband-to-be, her father Thomas was a Fellow at Oxford before his marriage; after it, he became a country vicar. In 1764, not long after her father first retired to Bath with his family, then promptly died, Cassandra married George Austen, after meeting him in Oxford.

> 'Mrs Morland was a very good woman, and wished to see her children everything they ought to be: but her time was so much occupied with lying-in and teaching the little ones, that her elder daughters were inevitably left to shift for themselves.'
>
> —*Northanger Abbey*, 1817

She was nearly 26, quite old for a first marriage at the time (Anne Elliot, the heroine of Austen's *Persuasion*, for example, is widely considered to be over the hill at just 28).

The union seems to have been a happy one. Although later in life she suffered from many maladies – some certainly real, but some imaginary, according to family lore – in youth and early middle age Cassandra was an indefatigable wife, bearing George Austen eight children while energetically running a busy household and a small school.

Above: Girls without helpful maternal guidance are a regular theme in Austen's books. In this Victorian illustration for *Northanger Abbey*, Catherine Morland is shown being led astray by Isabella Thorpe.

Opposite page: Handsome in youth, Mrs Austen's profile was rather hawkish by her old age when this silhouette was made.

A Fine Family

> 'We have now another girl, a present plaything for her sister Cassy and a future companion. She is to be Jenny, and seems to me as if she would be as like Henry, as Cassy is to Neddy.'
>
> —George Austen to Mrs Walter, 17 December 1775

James, the Austens' first child, was born the year after their marriage, and across the next decade they had six more, with a last son finally completing their family of eight in 1779. All lived to adulthood – extremely unusual at the time – and all but one were healthy. The second son, George, had a problem which was never diagnosed; he had seizures and may have suffered from epilepsy. He would eventually be sent to be looked after with an older invalid uncle, a brother of Mrs Austen, his father philosophically remarking that at least such a child could not grow up bad or wicked. The other seven siblings, with 14 years between the oldest and the youngest, grew up at Steventon.

Care in the Village

The Austen parents took a practical approach to parenthood: from the age of about three months, their babies were sent to a family in the nearby village who cared for them until they were toddlers, at which point they returned to the family home. Their parents probably visited them regularly, but the arrangement sounds odd today. It wasn't uncommon at the period, though, and it got over the difficulty of caring for small babies with so many other calls on Mrs Austen's time. The Reverend George wrote

to Mrs Walter, his half-brother's wife, that, as a result, the children 'turned all their little affections towards those who were about them and good to them...' without depending particularly on their mother. Nonetheless, it must have fractured the mother/baby bond, not much considered in an era when children were frequently brought up away from their parents for all kinds of reasons.

Jane was the second-to-last child – she had five older brothers, James, George, Edward, Henry and Francis, an older sister, Cassandra, and finally Charles, four years younger. She was born in the exceptionally harsh winter of 1775. George Austen mentions it without much fanfare in another letter to Mrs Walter, written the day after the birth – it was Mrs Austen's seventh confinement and although it came later than expected (she may have miscalculated her dates), it passed off without problems. She may have had her sister-in-law, Philadelphia, to stay and help her through labour, as she had at Cassandra's birth. Despite his prediction, and George's list of his children's nicknames, 'Jenny' never came to pass; the whole family knew her as Jane.

Below: The Austen family's eight children. Unusually for the 18th century, all survived into adulthood.

Opposite page: In the 1770s Steventon Rectory was a comfortable family home, with a sweep for carriages leading up the front door. Sadly, it was demolished in 1824.

Steventon, Hampshire

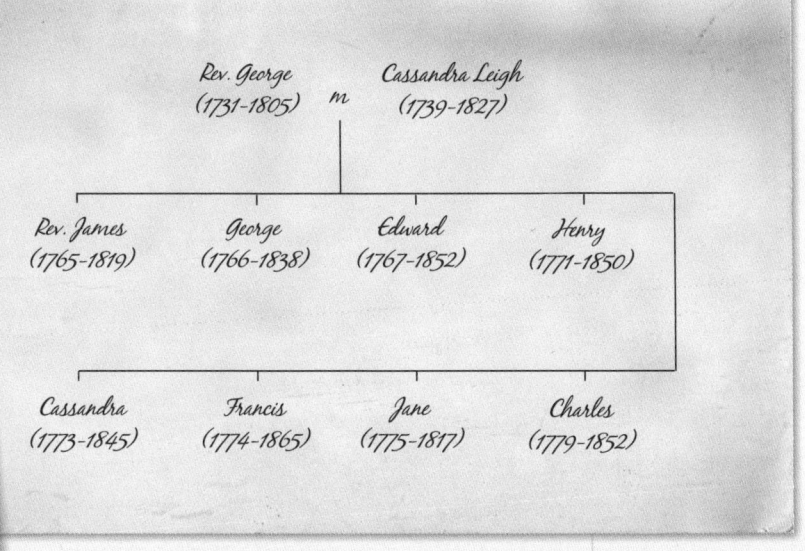

Making a Living

> *'I fear George will find it easier to get a family than to provide for them.'*
>
> —Tysoe Saul Hancock, George Austen's brother-in-law, writing to his wife Philadelphia, 1773

After their marriage and the acquisition of two Hampshire parishes, George and Cassandra Austen rented a small house at Deane, but their household rapidly outgrew it. In 1768, already with a family of three small boys and with a fourth child expected, they moved to Steventon Rectory in George's second parish, which was larger, though notoriously dank. Steventon remained the family base for 32 years; Jane lived there until she was 25.

Keeping a Family

A small country parish in the late 18th century was rarely a particularly profitable concern and doubling up, or pluralism, was often the only way to keep a vicar in situ. George Austen held services in both his parishes (Deane consisted of only around 24 families and, with 33, Steventon was not much larger), and officiated at christenings, weddings and funerals whenever needed. 'Vicaring' such small parishes didn't take up a huge amount of his time; he also farmed the land around Steventon and, with his wife, ran a small at-home school for the sons of the gentry, to bring in additional income. When he arrived in Hampshire it's estimated that his income would have been around £200 per year – barely enough for a large and growing family – although by the time he retired, it was closer to £600. Even this increase meant only that the Austens were modestly comfortable; they were certainly not rich.

"*I hope Mr. Bingley will like it, Lizzy.*"

Left: In *Pride and Prejudice*, the Bennet girls know that to secure comfortable futures they will need to marry money.

How Much Was Enough?

There's no shortage of mentions of income in Austen's novels. In *Pride and Prejudice*, Mr Bingley, with around £4,000 per year, is the big catch of the neighbourhood at the Netherfield ball, but is shortly eclipsed by his friend, Mr Darcy, who, with an annual income of £10,000, is very wealthy indeed. Heiresses were more likely to inherit a single sum than property – for example, both Darcy's sister, Georgiana, and Emma Woodhouse, heroine of *Emma*, will have £30,000 on marriage. All four are seriously rich.

At the other end of the scale, Elizabeth Bennet and her sisters can expect only around £50 per year after their father dies. When the youngest, Lydia, runs off with dashing but unprincipled Captain Wickham, her family know that this meagre inheritance won't tempt him into marriage with her, and it is left to Darcy to stump up the necessary.

As an adult, Jane Austen knew about money and was unconstrained in discussing it, as only those who don't have much can. Her circumstances were never desperate, but she clearly learned strict budgeting and small economies from childhood. Money could be inherited, earned or married into, and even the modest amount Austen earned in her lifetime was enough to make a difference to her style of living.

'He only wanted to aggrandise and enrich himself; and if Miss Woodhouse of Hartfield, the heiress of thirty thousand pounds, were not quite so easily obtained as he had fancied, he would soon try for Miss Somebody else with twenty, or with ten.'

—Emma Woodhouse reflects on her rejected suitor, Mr Elton, and his mercenary courtship, *Emma*, 1815

The Family Network

An enduring myth was to grow up around Jane Austen's life, probably fed first by the bland memoir published in 1869 by her nephew, James Edward Austen-Leigh. It maintained that she had lived in near retirement, with modest influences, tirelessly scribbling in her little notebooks. Only the last part of this was true. Although Jane would never travel outside England, her outlook was much less limited than the picture Austen-Leigh painted.

'We did not think of her as clever, still less as being famous; but we valued her as one always kind, sympathising, and amusing.'

—James Edward Austen-Leigh, feeding the rather mild – and patronising – view of Austen that became popular in the Victorian period, 1869

James Edward Austen-Leigh

A MEMOIR
OF
JANE AUSTEN
BY HER NEPHEW
J. E. AUSTEN LEIGH

THIRD EDITION
TO WHICH IS ADDED
LADY SUSAN
AND FRAGMENTS OF
TWO OTHER UNFINISHED TALES BY MISS AUSTEN

LONDON
RICHARD BENTLEY AND SON
NEW BURLINGTON STREET
Publishers in Ordinary to Her Majesty
1872

Philadelphia Hancock
1730-1792

Eliza Hancock
1761-1813

WHO WERE JANE AUSTEN'S GENTRY?

Most of the Austen family's connections would have come into the category of 'gentry' but within that, their social and financial range was considerable. In Elizabeth Bennet's face-off with Lady Catherine de Bourgh, for example, she describes Darcy as a 'gentleman' and herself as a 'gentleman's daughter'. Despite the massive disparity in their fortunes, 'so far we are equal', she argues, implying that there is nothing against the two marrying. 'But who was your mother?' retorts Lady Catherine, smartly hitting on the core of the problem, which is Mrs Bennet's embarrassing vulgarity.

Family Connections

First, there were the families of her mother and father. George and Cassandra Austen were both educated with broad interests and extensive connections, including lawyers, academics and churchmen – while they didn't have much money, they knew a wide range of people.

In the direct family, Mr Austen's sister, Philadelphia, and her daughter, Eliza, had lives closely entwined with those of his children, and would offer plenty of insights into their eventful lives, first in India and, later, in revolutionary France, where Eliza's husband would be guillotined during the Terror. Jane's earliest writings show a taste for the dramatic that may well have been fed by Philadelphia's experiences.

Even closer to home, Jane's brothers pursued energetic careers. Frank and Charles, both of whom went into the navy and rose through the ranks to admiral and rear admiral respectively, served as far afield as the Far East and the West Indies. In *Mansfield Park*, Fanny's brother William tells spirited anecdotes of life aboard ship, while *Persuasion* is filled with descriptions of naval men and their adventures at sea. Henry, the brother Jane was closest to, had a range of livelihoods, first joining the local militia, then becoming a banker, and ultimately a clergyman. Finally, her brother Edward's adoption into the rich Knight family would ensure that his two sisters had first-hand experience of the grand-establishment lifestyle that Jane used to draw her pictures of Pemberley and Mansfield Park.

Opposite page: James Edward Austen-Leigh published a memoir of his famous aunt, along with the manuscripts of *The Watsons* and *Lady Susan*.

Life at Steventon

The Austen parents lived busy lives. Apart from the demands of the small school they ran from home as a moneymaking enterprise, housekeeping in the late 18th and early 19th centuries would have involved plenty of hard work – the lady of the house would oversee and often be hands-on with numerous household jobs. Daughters would be expected to do their part, but even on a very modest income there would have been several servants to help, some visiting, some live-in.

THE ALL-IMPORTANT PARSONAGE

Jane Austen loved a parsonage: of all the houses in her novels, it is the descriptions of these that feel most familiar. And there are plenty of them; in *Emma*, Emma goes as far as to break her shoelace to force a visit to Mr Elton's parsonage, so that her idiotic little friend Harriet can look at his 'improvements' (Harriet has hopes of Mr Elton, but Mr Elton has hopes of Emma). The newly married Elinor and Edward's move into the parsonage is part of the happy ending of *Sense and Sensibility* (Colonel Brandon has generously paid for its decoration). Most memorably of all, the dreadful Mr Collins in *Pride and Prejudice* has a handsome parsonage to offer Charlotte Lucas at Hunsford, which she considers fair reward for marrying him – when Charlotte shows Elizabeth around it, the reader feels that they, too, are getting a thorough house tour.

Left: Engraving of typical parsonage life (this example from the Isle of Wight). Parents and children play genteelly in front of a spruce-thatched rectory while a hardworking gardener sweeps up behind them. The church is just visible in the background.

Daily Routines

At Steventon, George Austen spent time in his study, a pleasant room with a bay window, where he wrote sermons and organised farm work with John Bond, his bailiff. For some years the family kept a carriage which was used for visiting and any necessary pastoral care (in such a rural neighbourhood it was hard to do without one), but the carriage horses doubled up ploughing and doing other farm work as necessary. Mrs Austen had baking, cooking and laundry to oversee, plus clothes making and mending to organise. Most households had a stillroom where household cures and potions were made, and in addition there would be bottling and preserving, poultry- and beekeeping, as well as running the dairy – the Austens kept cows.

'We plan on having a steady cook and a young, giddy housemaid, with a sedate, middle-aged man, who is to undertake the double office of husband to the former and sweetheart to the latter.'

—Jane Austen, not taking the servants seriously, to Cassandra, 3 January 1801

Below Stairs

No genteel family managed the household work without help. While named servants make only occasional appearances in Austen's texts, even unnamed ones ensure the reader is aware of a whole separate world being lived alongside that of the novels' protagonists. In her modest parsonages, they provide an additional backdrop (and unheard commentary) to events. When Lydia shockingly elopes in *Pride and Prejudice*, and her mother goes into hysterics on hearing the news, Elizabeth asks Jane 'was there a servant… who did not know the whole story before the end of the day?' Of course the answer is no; when Lydia reappears, belatedly married, far from being embarrassed about her situation, she rushes off to show her ring to the Longbourn housekeeper and the two housemaids – a further marker of her shamelessness.

Early Reading

What did Jane Austen grow up reading? A variety of things: for a country parson, George Austen had an extensive collection – more than 500 books – and the whole family were keen readers and seem to have been given the run of their father's library. The younger Austens, including Jane, were probably taught to read by their mother, starting with alphabet books and graduating to works like *The History of Little Goody Two-Shoes*, a highly moral storybook first published in 1765.

She was clearly fluent while still very young. One of the first books we know she owned herself was in French: a copy of La Fontaine's *Fables Choisies*, possibly given to her as an eighth birthday present by her older cousin Eliza de Feuillide. Her name appears on the flyleaf with the date, 5 December 1793. She had already been away at school, and was expected to manage some French as well as to read English. *Fables Choisies* is well-thumbed and the back pages have the sort of scribbles all children make in their books – 'I wish I had done', says one, and 'Mothers angry father's gone out' another.

LIBRARY BOOKS

Books were expensive in Austen's time. One cheaper way to read them was to subscribe to a circulating library, which bought the latest titles and passed them around to members in return for a small fee. We know that Jane Austen used them when she lived in Bath and Southampton. She also bought novels by subscription (whereby the author was paid upfront before the book was printed); in 1795, when she was 20, her name appears on the subscription list for *Camilla*, by then-fashionable novelist Fanny Burney (pictured above), for which she paid a guinea.

Discovering Novels

As she grew up, Jane will have read a mixture of poetry, essays, plays, history, philosophy and novels – without a full record of George Austen's library we can't know for certain, but family history and her own work show that she was familiar with the essays of Dr Johnson and the poems of William Cowper, among plenty of others.

Novels weren't always highly regarded in Austen's day – she would get a whole book, *Northanger Abbey*, out of the fashion for lurid plots – although the Austens, no literary snobs, enjoyed them. She read the works of Fielding, Laurence Sterne and Charlotte Smith (the wildly popular chick lit novelist of her time). Her nephew remembered that the works of Samuel Richardson were favourites of her youth, especially *Sir Charles Grandison*, Richardson's last novel, published in 1754 and already well known by the time she would have been old enough to read it. In *Northanger Abbey*, shallow Isabella Thorpe dislikes Jane's own favourite: 'That [*Sir Charles Grandison*] is an amazing horrid book is it not? I remember Miss Andrews could not get through the first volume.' It turns out that the 'horridness' of Richardson's work lies in it being too worthy, whereas the contrasting 'horrid' list drawn up by Isabella is fashionably sensational, without Richardson's moral heft.

Below: Seeking out riches in the library. Jane's father had an unusual number and range of books for a man of modest means; they were an expensive luxury in the 18th and early 19th centuries.

Opposite page: La Fontaine's moral stories would have been considered ideal fare for young minds – children could brush up on their behaviour while improving their French.

"I will read you their names directly... Castle of Wolfenbach, Clermont, Mysterious Warnings, Necromancer of the Black Forest, Midnight Bell, Orphan of the Rhine, and Horrid Mysteries. Those will last us some time."

"Yes, pretty well;" [says Catherine] "but are they all horrid, are you sure they are all horrid?"

—Isabella Thorpe puts together a melodramatic reading list for the teenage Catherine Morland, *Northanger Abbey*, 1817

The School at Home

THE COST OF EDUCATION Scholars looking at the records of George Austen's Hoares bank account have worked out that the going rate for a pupil at Steventon in 1773 seems to have been around £35 per year; 20 years later, this had almost doubled to £65. By comparison, Mrs La Tournelle, who ran one of the schools that Jane and Cassandra attended, charged £35 for each pupil, so sending their daughters to school may not have been an economy for the Austens.

A small school offering homely surroundings and a good, basic education for a few boys was a way for an impecunious vicar to make ends meet and in 1773, two years before Jane was born, her parents began to take in a handful of pupils at Steventon. With an excellent education of his own, George Austen was well placed to teach, with his wife in charge of the pupils' pastoral care. It must have worked; the school lasted for over 20 years, until 1796. With five brothers at home on and off in her early childhood and attic bedrooms full of schoolboys, Jane Austen will have been very used to boys – their habits, interests, games and, sometimes, teasing. The family were only alone during holiday times – at Christmas and midsummer, when the pupils went home.

Below left: A 'dame' school, where younger children learned to read and write. The Austen school had pupils across a wide range of ages.

Below centre: A hornbook, with upper- and lower-case alphabets carved onto a thin sheet of animal horn, was a common aid for teaching children their letters.

Social Connections

The pupils at Steventon came from various backgrounds, although all would have been considered gentry. The most aristocratic was Lord Lymington, heir to the Duke of Portsmouth, although he did not last long – he arrived when he was only five, and Mrs Austen noted that her sons James and Edward enjoyed playing with him, but his mother took him away just a few months later because his speech was not developing as it should (he seems to have had some mental problems and later became noted as an eccentric and a sadist). While his stay was not a success, a number of other pupils and their families became lifelong friends of the Austens. One family in particular, the Fowles, sent four brothers there at different times; the second son, Tom Fowle, was a close friend of James Austen's and would eventually become engaged to Cassandra Austen, although he died before they could marry.

Mrs Austen paid close attention to the students' wellbeing, sometimes communicating with them in witty rhymes. One year she wrote in verse to Gilbert East, who had overstayed his Christmas holiday, to encourage his return to Steventon – he must have valued it, because he kept it in his papers. The last verse reads:

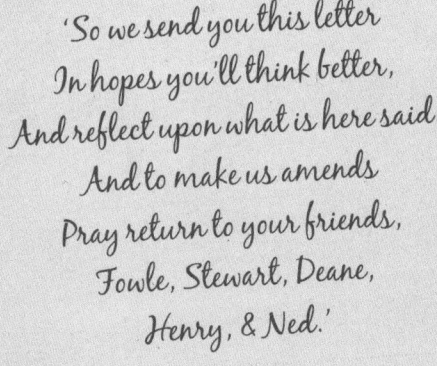

'So we send you this letter
In hopes you'll think better,
And reflect upon what is here said:
And to make us amends
Pray return to your friends,
Fowle, Stewart, Deane,
Henry, & Ned.'

Sent Away

'A real, honest, old-fashioned boarding school, where a reasonable quantity of accomplishments were sold at a reasonable price, and where girls might be sent to be out of the way and scramble themselves into a little education, without any danger of coming back prodigies.'

—Mrs Goddard's school, where Harriet Smith is a pupil, *Emma*, 1815

Jane Austen was only seven when she had her first taste of school in 1783: her cousin, Jane Cooper, was to be sent to a school in Oxford that had been started by Mrs Cawley, a widowed sister-in-law of Mrs Austen, and it was decided that Cassandra and Jane would keep her company. Not much is recorded of their months at Oxford; later in the year when there was a bad measles outbreak there, Mrs Cawley transplanted the school to Southampton – only to suffer an outbreak of typhus. All three girls seem to have been extremely ill, but Mrs Cawley didn't let the Austen or Cooper parents know – however, Jane Cooper wrote to her mother and the cousins were collected and taken home. Although the girls slowly recovered, Mrs Cooper caught the disease and died from it.

The Second School Experience

Despite this unhappy experience, the three girls were sent away again in the summer of 1785, this time to the Reading Ladies Boarding School. This may have been the model for Mrs Goddard's school in *Emma*. Mrs La Tournelle, the principal – real name, Sarah Hackitt – does not appear to have had much learning herself, although she did have an intriguing false leg made from cork. The school sounds like an easy-going place, where the pupils could 'scramble themselves into a little education'. Jane and Cassandra were visited there by their brother Edward, as well as by the Reverend Leigh, a cousin of their mother's. It may have been Leigh's visit that alerted the Austens that their girls weren't learning much, prompting their removal in 1786; from then on, they were kept at home.

Economics

The decision to send the girls to school may have been pragmatic – to make way for more paying pupils at Steventon. Another family event that was probably decided on economic grounds was the adoption of the Austens' son Edward in 1783 by George Austen's rich cousins – the family who had given him the living at Steventon – Thomas and Catherine Knight. Childless themselves, they had carried Edward off on various visits before formally adopting him when he was 15 years old. Years later, Henry Austen remembered that his father had misgivings about giving Edward up, and it was his mother who had gently urged him, saying 'I think, my dear, you had better oblige your cousins and let the child go.' Handing a child over to richer relations was not uncommon at the time – in *Emma*, Jane Austen would write Frank Churchill into a similar situation: indulged, but living at the whim of his rich, hypochondriacal aunt.

Above: An 1803 watercolour of the Abbey Gateway in Reading, once part of the Reading Ladies Boarding School, run by the eccentric Mrs La Tournelle.

Opposite page: Oxford High Street – known simply as the High – as Jane would have seen it when she arrived at Mrs Cawley's school in the city.

Indian Influence and French Glamour

> *'She is not the first Girl to have gone to the East Indies for a Husband'*
>
> —From *Catharine, or the Bower*, juvenilia by Jane Austen

O f all the wider family who brought outside influences into the vicar's household at Steventon, Mr Austen's sister Philadelphia and her daughter Eliza were the most exotic.

The Adventuring Aunt

Like her brother, Phila had been cast adrift early and was apprenticed to a London milliner at 15; in 1752, seeing no desirable future in England, she became an early member of the 'fishing fleet', the nickname for impecunious young ladies who sailed to India, then full of single men in want of wives. Her mission was successful: shortly after her arrival in Madras she married an older man – a surgeon with the then all-powerful East India Company, Tysoe Saul Hancock.

The Hancocks were friendly with Warren Hastings, the future Governor General of Bengal, and his wife, Marian. When Hastings was looking for care for his sickly young son George, Phila suggested he be entrusted to the care of her brother in England and his new wife, and the

'She was a clever woman, and highly accomplished, after the French rather than the English mode... such an element in the society of a country parsonage must have been a rare acquisition... She also took principal parts in the private theatricals in which the family several times indulged'

—Eliza de Feuillide, described by James Edward Austen-Leigh; *Memoir of Jane Austen*, 1869

child was shipped over to the care of George and Cassandra. He died shortly afterwards, but his brief period with the Austens cemented the link between the families. Phila's daughter Eliza's real father may have been Warren Hastings, who was a widower by the time she was born – he was her godfather and would later settle a considerable fortune on her – but although there was plenty of speculation on the subject, her paternity remains uncertain.

Eliza in England

Eliza and her mother returned to England in 1765. Hancock remained in India; when he died 10 years later Phila and Eliza moved to France where it was cheaper to live, and where, aged just 20, Eliza married the Comte de Feuillide in Paris. At 25 she came on a visit to her English relations at Steventon with her mother and her infant son – Jane was 11, and Eliza must have seemed a figure of impossible glamour to her country cousin. She had delicate good looks and dressed in high style, she had spent time at the court at Versailles and she excelled at the family theatricals that the young Austens loved. Both James and Henry Austen formed strong feelings for her, but it was Henry she would eventually marry after her first husband was guillotined during the French revolution.

Jane remained fond of and close to Eliza. And while the latter may not have been the exact model for any specific character, critics have speculated that both the amoral Lady Susan in Austen's early work and the alluring Mary Crawford in *Mansfield Park* have elements of Eliza's worldly side. Mary Crawford in particular is convincing in a way that might have been harder for Jane Austen to write without her experience of her cousin.

Above: Warren Hastings, Governor General of Bengal, on horseback, from an original painted by George Stubbs in 1796.

Opposite page: A family portrait of the Hancocks by Joshua Reynolds, painted in 1765. Four-year-old Eliza stands centre stage, supported by her mother and her Indian *ayah*, Clarinda.

Literary Entertainments

Below: A 1790 etching satirising the fashion for private performances. One player is making the most of *Jane Shore*, a popular tragedy. Meanwhile a monkey races up the bookshelves, a cat and dog squabble, a servant spills coals all over the floor and on the far right – shades of *Mansfield Park*? – some heavy flirtation is going on.

Opposite page: First performed in 1798, *Lovers' Vows* had a wildly successful run on the London stage, but its themes – seduction and illegitimacy among them – made it a highly unsuitable choice for the amateur theatricals in *Mansfield Park*.

The Steventon Theatre

The young Austens didn't just read; they also performed plays at home. The late 18th century saw a craze for private theatres among the aristocracy which gradually filtered down to the gentry; the Austen family were simply following the fashion. James Austen managed the performances, chose the plays and wrote their tailored introductions and epilogues. Jane was only seven at the time of the first production, *Matilda*, a tragedy set in Norman times with plenty of set-piece speeches; in subsequent years, there were performances of Sheridan's comedy *The Rivals*, *The Wonder* by Susanna Centlivre – which features plenty of romantic muddle and misunderstanding – and Henry Fielding's extravagant satire *The History of Tom Thumb the Great*. Later productions were moved from Steventon parlour to the barn, which had been fitted up with a proper stage and curtains.

A Literary Catalyst?

In 1787, when the home performances were well established, Jane Austen began writing in earnest. Some of her juvenilia were in the form of plays, and the excitement around the home theatre seems to have sparked her creativity; she was to write her way through her teens.

A PRIVATE REHEARSAL OF JANE SHORE.

Years later, she would call on her memories for *Mansfield Park* – in the novel, a play reading becomes a full-blown performance which compromises the performers, in particular Maria Bertram who is engaged to the dullard Mr Rushworth but has a strong fancy for the unscrupulous Henry Crawford. The play is one of Austen's finest set pieces; her quiet heroine Fanny Price expresses misgivings but, as the least important member of any Mansfield gathering, is shouted down. The play (the morally unsuitable *Lovers' Vows*) reveals the faults in every performer, and the fractures in their relationships. Austen had no doubt watched cousin Eliza acting her parts and flirting with the Austen brothers. And there's a level of detail in the Mansfield theatre that could only have come from direct experience – from the scenery knocked out by the estate carpenter to the covert 'private' rehearsals enjoyed by the would-be lovers.

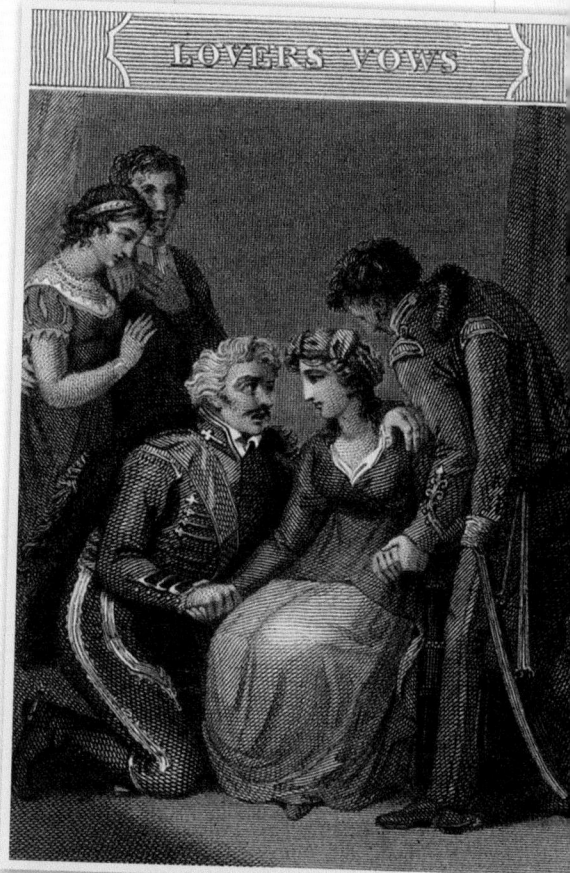

'You know we have long projected acting this Christmas... & this scheme would go on a vast deal better would you lend your assistance... on finding there were two unengaged parts I immediately thought of you... I am certain You will succeed in them.'

—Eliza de Feuillide urging her cousin Philly Walter to join the Steventon theatricals, 16 November 1787

CHAPTER TWO

BECOMING A WRITER

Early Writings

> *'To Madame La Comtesse de Feuillide This Novel is inscribed by her Obliged Humble Servant the Author. "Deceived in Freindship and Betrayed in Love"'*
>
> —Jane's extravagant dedication to *Love and Freindship*, 1790

If the thrill of home theatricals was the spark that ignited Jane Austen's own writing, once she started, she kept going. She carefully preserved her so-called juvenilia, written between the ages of 11 and 17, making fair copies into three vellum hard-bound notebooks, labelled 'Volume the First', 'Volume the Second' and 'Volume the Third' – an ironical nod to the presentation of contemporary novels, which came in multiple volumes. There's a note on the second notebook that it was a present from her father; given that they would have been expensive indulgences, it's likely that the others were, too.

Finding Her Voice

The contents of the books are standalone pieces and aren't in date order; they range from short playlets to comic stories, and a very condensed 'History of England' which is illustrated with watercolour portraits by Cassandra. Although Austen's first 'effusions' came in several different forms, from the outset their tone is bold and anarchic, a surprise for anyone who has a fixed idea of her as the author of drawing-room romances between ladies and gentlemen. Many of the pieces are dedicated to family members – they were probably read aloud, and the longer pieces may have been part works, with the chapters delivered as they were finished.

"Drove her into a fainting fit"
Chapter XXXVII

> 'Beware of fainting-fits... Run mad as often as you chuse; but do not faint.'
>
> —Good advice from *Love and Freindship*, 1790

Above: As a mature writer, Austen kept fainting fits to a minimum: in this late 19th-century illustration to *Sense and Sensibility*, though, Marianne's faint is completely in character.

These early heroes and heroines outrage convention. While some come to sticky ends, others triumph undeservedly. One of the shortest sets the tone: *The Beautifull Cassandra*, dedicated to Jane's sister, is the story of a marvellous day in which Cassandra steals a bonnet from her milliner mother, then parades around town, 'devouring' six ices at the Pastry Cook's and knocking him down when he pushes for payment. After several shocking incidents – Cassandra is good at causing chaos and running away – our heroine returns home and is embraced by her fond parent; her story consists of chapters of just a line or two each.

Longer pieces offer romances that dive from high emotion to bathetic conclusions; *Love and Freindship* (sic), written when Jane was 14, has a mock-elaborate dedication to Eliza de Feuillide, and takes the form of letters, like the then-fashionable epistolary novels. It makes fun of Gothic plots and attitudes (an idea that would come to fruition in *Northanger Abbey*) – full of young ladies whose frequent fainting fits don't usually work out to their advantage.

It's clear that Jane Austen enjoyed writing from the very beginning. Over time she would curb her wildest flights of self-expression, but her merciless eye for the ridiculous and the affected would serve her well in all her adult novels.

Reading Aloud

'To hear those beautiful lines which have frequently driven me almost wild, pronounced with such impenetrable calmness, such dreadful indifference!'

—Marianne Dashwood finding fault with Edward Ferrars' reading, *Sense and Sensibility*, 1811

Reading aloud well was admired in Austen's time, an art on a par with being able to play a musical instrument to entertain friends and neighbours, and it was one practised by all the Austens at home. James, 10 years Jane's senior, was acknowledged as 'literary' and probably led the way, encouraged by both his bookish parents. It was a social skill – just compare Marianne Dashwood's irritation at hearing a work by her (and Jane Austen's) favourite poet Cowper read aloud in a dull fashion by Edward Ferrars, her sister's beau, in *Sense and Sensibility* with the reluctant but true admiration Fanny Price feels when Henry Crawford – her own unwanted suitor – reads Shakespeare skilfully in *Mansfield Park*, acting out the characters: '… in Mr Crawford's reading there was a variety of excellence beyond what she had ever met with'. Even the indolent Lady Bertram admires Crawford's skill – '…it was really like being at a play!' In a world in which home entertainments were limited to conversation, making music, perhaps with some dancing, and reading, such a performer was an asset.

Austen as Performer

In Georgian society, girls were less likely to be taught to declaim than boys, and generally girls acting, even in a private production, was considered not quite respectable – but the Austen family circle was dominated by boys and boys' interests, and it's clear that, encouraged by her parents, Jane enjoyed acting out her writing and reading aloud.

Later she would read her novels, while still works in progress, to a few chosen family members, and sometimes to friends, too – in which case, they might not be told she was the author. She enjoyed hearing their unrestrained comments, unaware that they were listening to her own work. A good performer herself, she would be quick to criticise those less talented (reporting on one early reading of *Pride and Prejudice* to neighbours, she remarked that her mother's slow reading had lessened her audience's enjoyment).

Above: Reading aloud to the family circle – a popular diversion while the women of the household got on with the endless sewing needed to keep everyone decently clothed.

Opposite page: A gifted reader like Henry Crawford could keep their audience enthralled at a time when families had to devise their own home entertainments.

'She read aloud with very great taste and effect. Her own works, probably, were never heard so much to advantage as from her own mouth.'

—Henry Austen recalls Jane's reading in his 'Biographical Notice of the Author' written for the first publication of *Northanger Abbey*, 1817

Paper and Ink

LEARNING TO READ

First lessons in recognising letters and starting to shape them weren't radically different in the 18th century from those children learn today. A child might begin with alphabet blocks or letters written on squares of card; when they graduated to writing, they would often practise with a pencil – much easier than a quill – onto paper ruled into lines by an adult.

Jane Austen wrote in an elegant flowing copperplate which can only have been the result of long hours of childhood practice. The business of writing was time consuming, but it was a key skill, because letters were the only means of communicating with someone at any distance.

The Mechanics of Writing

Once Austen could write, she needed to learn to manage a quill. Quill pens were usually made from the large feathers from the edge of a goose's wing, 'cured' in hot sand to harden them, and bought from the stationer's shop, along with paper. Ink might be homemade (there's a recipe for ink written by Martha Lloyd when she lived with the Austen women at Chawton) but could also be bought in the form of a powder to be mixed with water. A penknife for re-pointing the nib of a quill would usually be to hand. Someone like Austen who regularly wrote a lot might keep two or three quills on the go – as she wrote, the quill would absorb ink, gradually soften and begin to produce an irregular line, at which point she could take up a fresh one, leaving the first to dry out and harden, ready to be used again.

The paper would also need something soft, usually a felt pad, to rest on as she wrote – too hard a surface would stress the quill and wear it out quickly. Quills and ink were relatively cheap but paper was expensive, made by hand, from rags, and cut into sheets. You could buy a single sheet, but the usual domestic purchase would be a packet of perhaps two dozen. Writing paper was dipped in size to give it a smooth surface, helping to avoid blots.

Revealing Letters

In *Pride and Prejudice*, the letter Miss Bingley sends Jane Bennet to announce the family's departure from Netherfield carries signs of her social superiority. The paper she uses is expensive – smooth and easy to write on – and the letter is contained in an outer wrapper, an extravagant waste of a sheet of paper when most everyday letters would consist of a sheet closely covered in writing and perhaps written in the other direction ('crossed') before being folded, with the address written on the only remaining blank quarter.

> *'The envelope contained a sheet of elegant, little hot-pressed paper, well covered in a lady's fair, flowing hand.'*
>
> —Miss Bingley's letter arrives at Longbourn, *Pride and Prejudice*, 1813

Right: Jane Bennet setting off to cement her friendship with the Bingley sisters at Netherfield, in a late 19th-century illustration for *Pride and Prejudice*.

Opposite page: Jane Austen wrote in a remarkably neat, flowing hand, especially given the temperamental nature of the 'pen' of the era: a goose-feather quill.

Close Friends

COUNTRY SOCIETY

Apart from their two short periods at boarding school, Jane and Cassandra's childhood and adolescence were lived mostly among boys, but as they became teenagers their social circle enlarged; they visited around the neighbourhood, attended the informal dances held locally and built more friendships with other girls.

Georgian country families socialised a good deal. When Mrs Bennet boasts of dining with 'four-and-twenty families' that sounds like a lot to modern ears, but it's clear that it would have seemed very limited indeed to a sophisticate like Mr Darcy (who has just commented on the limits of life in the country). The Austen sisters made some close female friends in their teens who accompanied them on their entry into country society, and to whom they would remain close all their lives.

Right: Jane and Cassandra working companionably in the Steventon garden, envisaged in 1904 by the illustrator Walter Paget.

Opposite page: Luxurious Manydown, home of the Bigg family. The Austen sisters were regular visitors to the handsome manor house, which was set in an extensive park.

The Lloyds and the Biggs

In 1789 two new families moved into the neighbourhood of Steventon. The first were the Lloyds, the impecunious widow of a clergyman and her three daughters, Martha, Mary and Eliza, who rented the parsonage at Deane from George Austen. Eliza soon married, and the family connection would eventually be strengthened – in 1797 – when Mary married James Austen, but although Mary was closer to Jane in age (Martha was a full 10 years older), Jane always preferred Martha and she would become her closest friend, moving in with Cassandra, Jane and their mother when they went to Chawton Cottage. Her connection with the family lasted even after Jane died; when she was in her sixties, in 1828, she made a late marriage to Francis Austen, five years after the death of his first wife.

At the other end of the social scale, the second family, the Biggs, moved into Manydown, a grand house about six miles from Steventon. This time the head of the family was a widower, Lovelace Bigg, who had seven children. Five were daughters, the three younger of whom would become close friends with the Austen girls. Alethea, Elizabeth and Catherine – Jane's particular friend – are frequently mentioned in letters, played an important part in neighbourhood society, and provided a reason and a base for Cassandra and Jane to visit even after the Austens left Steventon.

> *'...as to not meeting with many people in this neighbourhood, I believe there are few neighbourhoods larger. I know we dine with four-and-twenty families.'*

—Mrs Bennet struggles to impress Mr Darcy, *Pride and Prejudice*, 1813

The First Full Work

A short but complete novel, *Lady Susan* is the link between Austen's juvenilia and her mature work. Probably finished in 1794, it was unread outside the family until it was finally published by James Edward Austen-Leigh alongside his *Memoir of Jane Austen* in 1871. It's never become truly popular, but it's still well worth reading for the sake of its monstrous central character, Lady Susan Vernon.

A Villainous Anti-heroine

Jane Austen's famous comment about *Emma*, that 'I am going to take a heroine whom no one but myself will much like', proved false: readers quickly took to the well-meaning but misguided Emma Woodhouse. No one but a sociopath, though, could much like Lady Susan – she is gloriously immoral, subversive, cynical and bitchy. *Lady Susan* is interesting because it's a true in-between work. The plotting is lively and the action moves along briskly, but the author hasn't yet hit the fine gradations in tone that are so characteristic of her later books; everything is drawn with a much coarser brush.

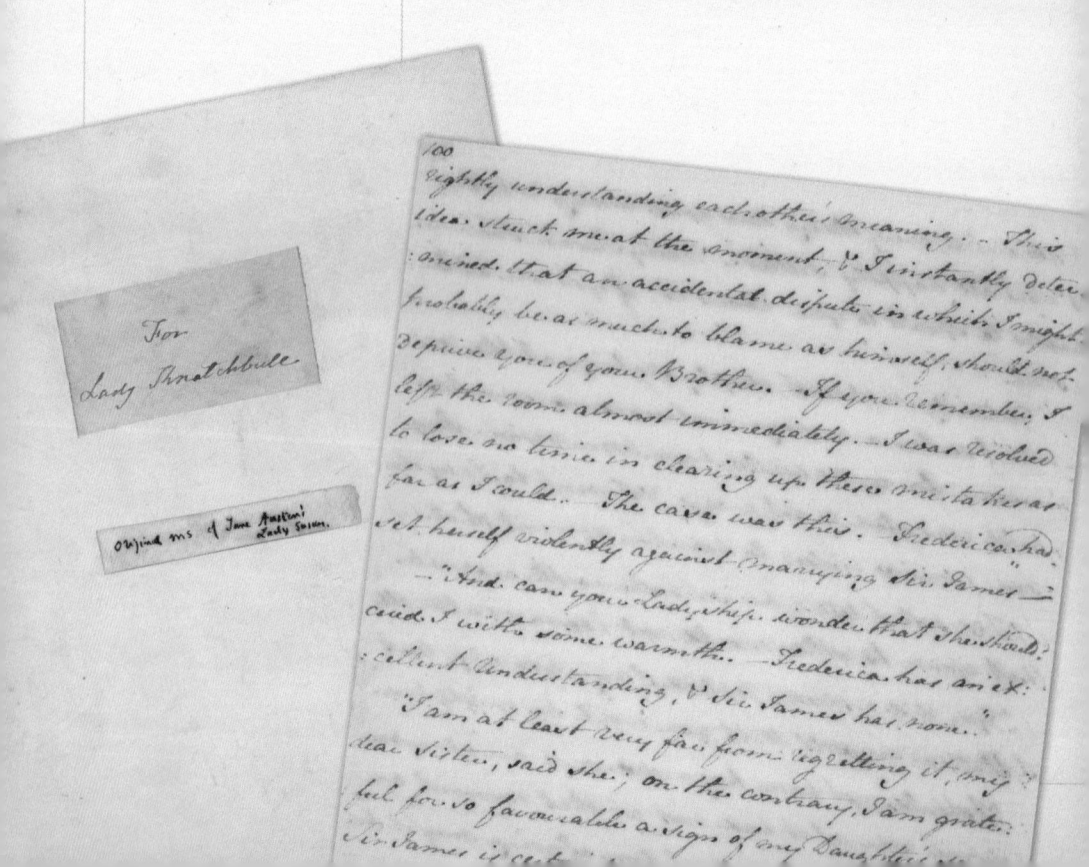

Below: The tidy version of the manuscript of *Lady Susan*, labelled 'For Lady Knatchbull' by Cassandra Austen. Cassandra distributed Jane's writings long after her death; Lady Knatchbull had been Fanny Knight, one of the sisters' favourite nieces, before her marriage.

Opposite page: Written around 1794, *Lady Susan* only finally made it into print in 1871.

Austen clearly valued the story as she did all her work – it survives as the only complete draft of any of her novels in her own hand. The watermarked paper it is written on dates it to 1805, so the copy must have been made long after she completed the original. It's an epistolary novel – that is, the text consists of exchanges of letters, a form that probably reached its peak in 1778 with the publication of Fanny Burney's wildly successful *Evelina*, a favourite with Jane, and which had dated by the turn of the century.

Breaking the Rules

The plot is more carefully worked out than those of her earlier pieces. A charming, beautiful but impecunious widow in her mid-thirties, Lady Susan is determined to marry advantageously herself, and to make sure her virtuous daughter Frederica does likewise, regardless of her own preference. And she spares no efforts to get the result she wants, whoever is deceived or made unhappy in the process.

Was any aspect of this anti-heroine taken from life? As with the sophisticated but heartless Mary Crawford, some scholars have pointed the finger – again – at Eliza de Feuillide, but there's no evidence that Austen borrowed anything but Eliza's sophistication: hardly surprising, as Eliza was probably the most worldly person that she knew. Lady Susan's most villainous qualities were probably drawn purely by Jane's imagination – an imagination which, as can be seen in her earliest works, was capable of running wild all on its own.

'Artlessness will never do in love matters'

—Lady Susan Vernon telling it how it is, *Lady Susan*, 1871

Lady Susan

I

Lady Susan Vernon to Mr. Vernon

Langford, Dec.

My DEAR BROTHER,—I can no longer refuse myself the pleasure of profiting by your kind invitation when we last parted of spending some weeks with you at Churchhill, and therefore, if quite convenient to you and Mrs. Vernon to receive me at present, I shall hope within a few days to be introduced to a sister whom I have so long desired to be acquainted with. My kind friends here are most affectionately urgent with me to prolong my stay, but their hospitable and cheerful dispositions lead them too much into society for my present situation and state of mind; and I impatiently look forward to the hour when I shall be admitted into your delightful retirement.

I long to be made known to your dear little children, in whose hearts I shall be very eager to secure an interest. I shall soon have need for

[3]

In Her Own Words

WHO DID JANE WRITE TO?
1796 is a good year for Austenites: it's the first time we hear her direct voice in a letter. While it's been calculated that Jane Austen wrote around 3,000 letters across her lifetime, only 160 survive, 95 of which were written to Cassandra. Of the remainder, most were sent to close family and friends, with just a handful going to her publishers and patrons.

Below: Thomas Langlois Lefroy would go on to be a family man with a successful career, eventually becoming Lord Chief Justice of Ireland. In old age he told a nephew that he had had a 'boyish love' for Jane Austen.

Opposite page: The first Austen letter that has survived, an energetic jumble of teasing, local gossip and shopping commissions.

Fittingly, the first letter we have is written to her sister, to mark the latter's 23rd birthday. It is dated 9/10 January; Jane was at home in Steventon, and Cassandra was spending the Christmas holidays with the Fowles, then her prospective in-laws, at Kintbury in Berkshire.

'Imagine to Yourself Everything Most Profligate...'

It's not a long letter, but it fits a lot in. Jane has been to a local ball the night before; she hoped to see Charles Fowle (one of the four Fowles who had attended the Steventon school, and the brother of Cassandra's fiancé) but he wasn't there. Someone who was there was Tom Lefroy, the young Irish lawyer, nephew of Jane's friend and mentor Madam Lefroy, who was visiting his aunt at nearby Ashe. The couple danced and sat out together in a 'profligate' way, and she has heard he is much teased about her at his hostess's house.

Lefroy has long been the subject of speculation for scholars and biographers – was he a serious attachment? The answer is almost certainly no, despite Jane's giddy mentions of him – both parties knew that their attraction couldn't develop given that neither had the money to marry. The most striking thing for anyone reading the letter is how young its author sounds – Lefroy may simply represent the potential for exciting developments. Readers accustomed to Austen as narrator, in control of her plots, quickly realise that this is something different, a letter written by a girl, just 21, with a wide acquaintance and plenty of dance partners, alert to the possibility of romantic attachment.

'... I am almost afraid to tell you how my Irish friend and I behaved... in the way of dancing and sitting out together.'

—Letter from Jane to Cassandra, boasting of 'shocking' behaviour with Tom Lefroy at the local ball, 9 January 1796

Other Topics

The letter also rapidly ranges over a visit from brother Henry – who was considering the purchase of a lieutenancy – and his friend; the modish 'illumination' of the greenhouse at the ball, and whether or not the aforementioned Charles Fowle will carry out Austen's commission in town for some new silk stockings (if he does buy them, she worries that she doesn't have the funds to pay him). There is a tiny, chilly echo of Jane at her most sardonic at the very end: 'I am sorry for the Beaches' loss of their little girl', she writes, 'especially as it is the one so much like me.'

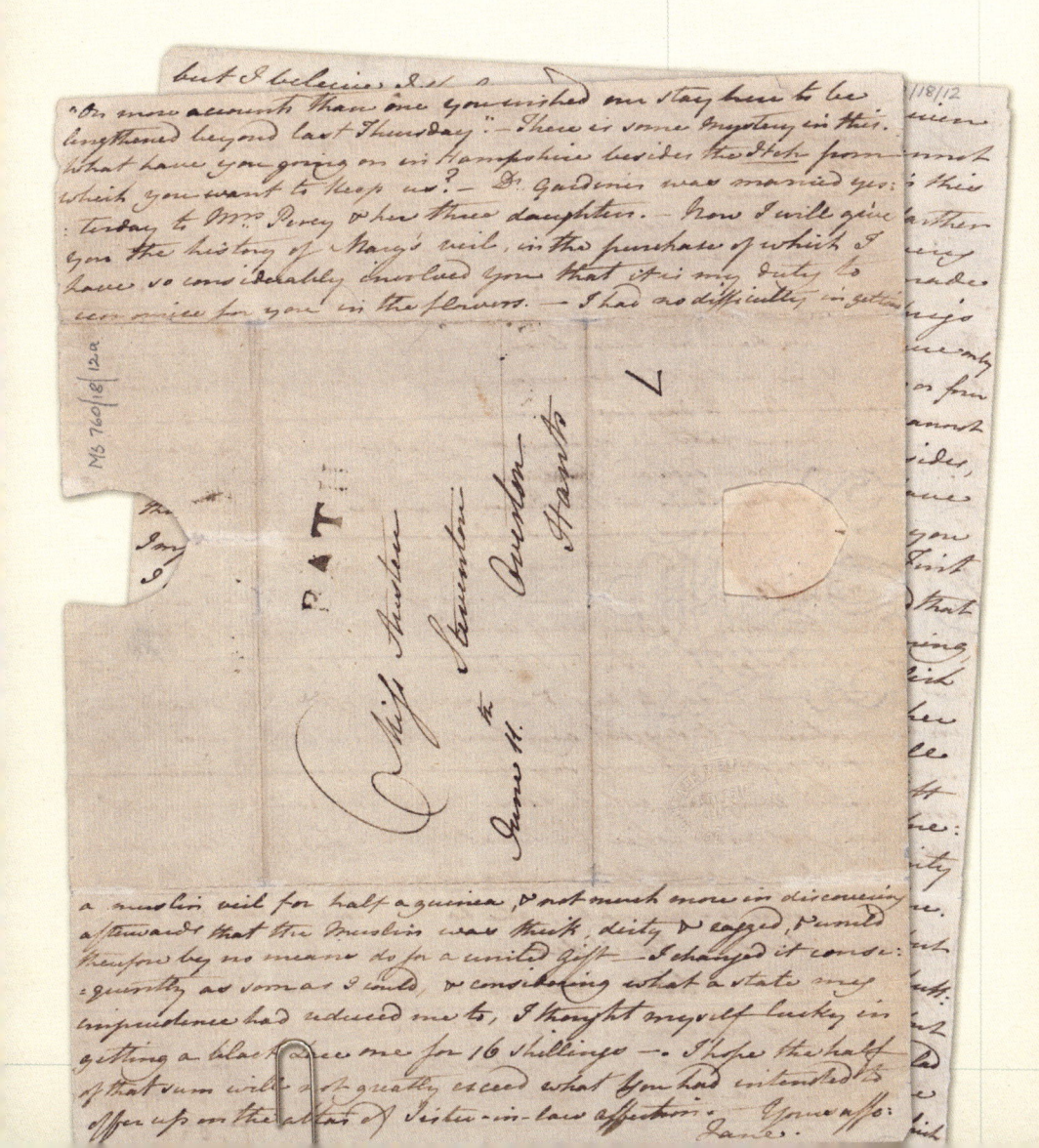

Army, Navy and Church

SUITABLE PROFESSIONS
Apart from lucky Edward, in line to inherit substantial estates due to his adoption, and disabled George, who was looked after away from Steventon and is hardly mentioned in family records, the Austen sons needed professions, and all were well embarked on their chosen careers by the time we have the first letter from Jane.

James, Jane's oldest brother, was considered 'literary'; he led the theatricals at Steventon and, while still at Oxford, started a short-lived periodical, *The Loiterer*. Like his father, he opted for the Church and was ordained in 1789. After three years of marriage, his wife, Anne Mathew, died suddenly in 1792, leaving a small daughter, Anna, a favourite with her Steventon aunts. In 1797 he would marry Mary Lloyd, and after George Austen's retirement in 1800 the couple moved into the house at Steventon, and James replaced his father as the parish's clergyman.

Edward Austen-Knight took an extensive Grand Tour, the mark of moneyed young gentlemen, and in 1791 married a suitably beautiful girl, Elizabeth Bridges, who would bear him 11 children. When Mr Knight senior died in 1794, Edward became heir to his estates, and eventually moved into his grand house, Godmersham, where his sisters would be regular visitors.

Right: A portrait of Edward Austen Knight aged 21, painted to mark his Grand Tour and full of appropriate references, including classical ruins.

Opposite top: Godmersham Park, main Kent residence of the Knight family, regularly visited by all the Austen siblings.

Opposite bottom: An officer of the 52nd Regiment, shown in the red coat that was such a focus of admiration for Austen's younger Bennet sisters. Henry Austen's military career would last for eight years, until 1801.

The Army

Henry, the fourth son, is often called Jane's favourite brother, although he was also the one most likely to find himself in trouble – 'Oh, What a Henry!' is the exclamation famously attributed to his sisters. Originally destined for the Church, he joined the Oxfordshire militia in 1793 when war broke out with France, taking several leaves of absence, both to finish his degree and, in 1797, to marry Eliza de Feuillide. He eventually became regimental paymaster and used the experience to set up his next career, as a banker, in 1801. In 1816 he would go sensationally bankrupt and revert to his original career choice of clergyman. With Cassandra, he would act as Jane's literary executor.

'... though so highly gifted by Nature, my Uncle was not prosperous in life.'

—Henry, described by his niece, Anna, in the 1850s

The Navy

Frank and Charles, the youngest Austen brothers, entered the Royal Navy Academy in Portsmouth as 12-year-olds and rose rapidly in the ranks. By 1799 Frank was commanding officer of HMS *Peterel*; in 1863, he would achieve the ultimate rank of Admiral of the Fleet.

Charles, who would eventually become a rear admiral, joined his first ship, HMS *Daedalus*, at 15 in 1794, and had made the rank of lieutenant on HMS *Scorpion* by 1797.

The naval careers of her two youngest brothers supplied Jane with a mass of material which she would put to good use, both in *Mansfield Park* and, especially, in her last completed novel, *Persuasion*.

Visiting

Odd One Out
By the mid-1790s, all the Austen children were launched – James, Henry and Edward working and/or married, and Charles and Francis busy with their naval careers. Cassandra became engaged to Tom Fowle in 1794, although they could not marry because he did not yet have a living. For a few years, this left Jane as the odd one out.

She was now old enough to be looking for a husband, and it was at this point that girls were usually exposed to as wide a range of acquaintance as possible, often making long visits to relations in different parts of the country, at least partly in the hope that they would meet a suitable partner – rich enough, agreeable enough and all-round eligible enough to marry. Jane Austen was poor, and the only real security she could find would be in marriage.

On the Marriage Market
Cassandra and Jane attended the public assemblies at Basingstoke, near home, as teenagers. Plenty of their established circle went, and the dances were a 'soft' way of introducing girls into society. Frustratingly the absence of her letters before 1796, and their scarcity after – only 22 letters written between 1796 and the end of 1799 survive – can't give us her own view, but we know that she spent time in Southampton in 1793, visiting her father's cousin Elizabeth Butler-Harris, who was having a baby; that she paid visits to her mother's Leigh cousins in Adlestrop in Gloucestershire in 1794 and again in 1799, and that she spent November 1797 in Bath with her mother's rich brother, James Leigh Perrot, and his wife Jane.

I really believe if she had only a shilling in the world she would be very likely to give away sixpence of it

Rich Versus Poor

Much later in life Austen would describe the differences between rich and poor unmarried women in *Emma*. Rich Emma ridicules the impoverished and exhaustingly talkative spinster Miss Bates at the disastrous Box Hill picnic, and is rebuked by Mr Knightley on the grounds of their difference in status; when Emma herself declares that she won't marry to her friend, love-mad Harriet Smith, she points out that being a rich spinster, free from commitments, is not a bad position to be in.

We don't know what Austen's mother was inferring when she wrote to Mary Lloyd that Jane would be gone 'the Lord knows where', when her mother was old, but it sounds as though her expectation that Jane would do the conventional thing was already wearing thin.

Above: Miss Bates at the picnic at Box Hill, and giving to those with even less than herself – one of the poorest characters in the novels. Austen draws her, sometimes rather poignantly, as both benign and ridiculous.

Opposite page: A 1798 etching by Thomas Rowlandson of the – apparently rather clodhopping – pleasures of a public dance, here at the fashionable Bath Assembly Rooms.

'I look forward to you as a real comfort to me in my old age, when Cassandra is gone into Shropshire, & Jane – the Lord knows where.'

—Letter to Mary Lloyd from Cassandra Austen, Jane's mother, 30 November 1796

Mrs Lefroy

MENTOR
Other than members of her extended family and close friends such as Martha Lloyd and the Biggs girls, there was another particularly important person in young Jane Austen's life. This was Anne Lefroy, always known in the Steventon neighbourhood as Madam Lefroy, both on account of her personal sophistication, and possibly her Huguenot ancestry.

Anne was the wife of the Reverend George Lefroy, and the family lived at the rectory at Ashe, near Steventon, from the late 1770s. Twenty-six years older than Jane, she was an established young matron when Jane was still a child; they probably first met when the Austen girls were invited over as playmates for her own daughter. But the relationship that developed was between Anne herself and the Austens' younger daughter. A close friend and mentor, Anne seems sometimes to have even been something of a substitute mother, listening to confidences and offering advice. She was energetic, intellectually curious, a poet and well up on current books, with a library at Ashe that Jane could also borrow from.

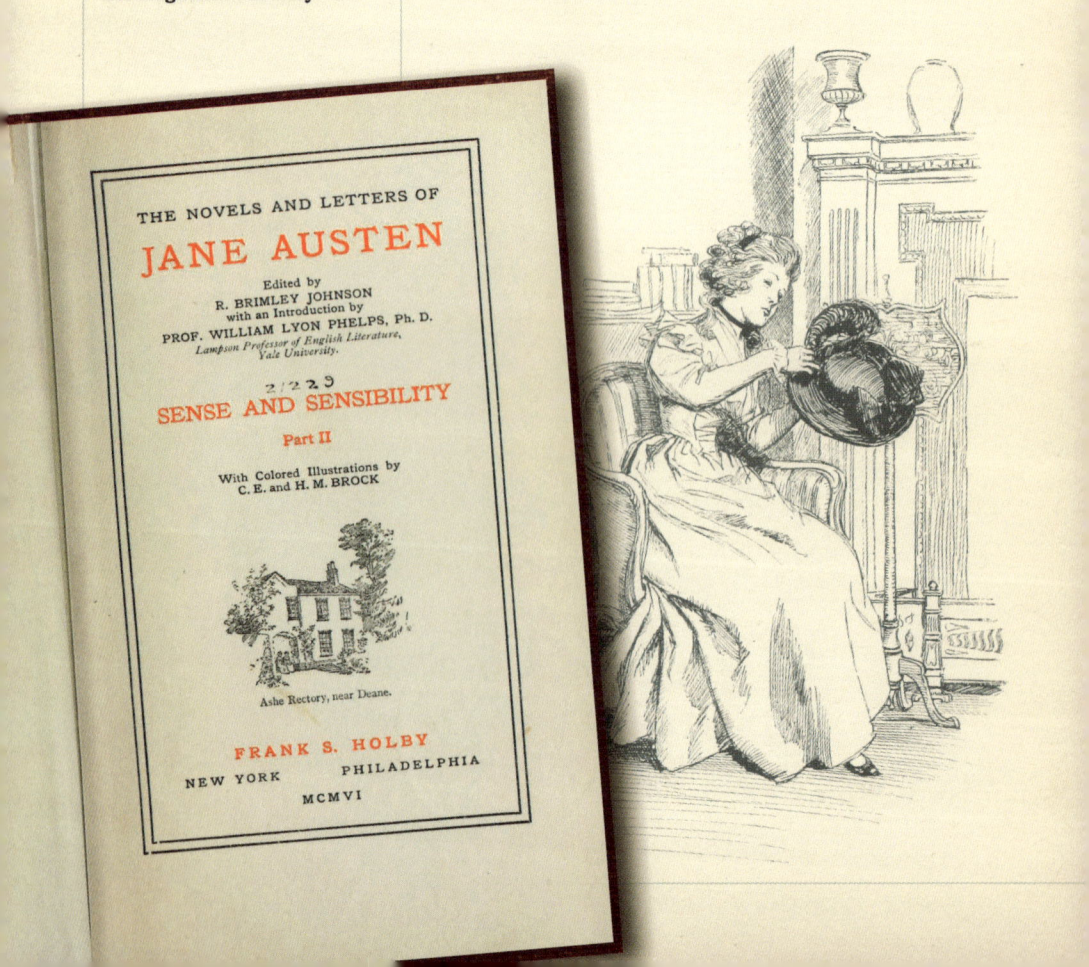

THE NOVELS AND LETTERS OF
JANE AUSTEN
Edited by
R. BRIMLEY JOHNSON
with an Introduction by
PROF. WILLIAM LYON PHELPS, Ph.D.
Lampson Professor of English Literature,
Yale University.

2/229

SENSE AND SENSIBILITY
Part II

With Colored Illustrations by
C. E. and H. M. BROCK

Ashe Rectory, near Deane.

FRANK S. HOLBY
NEW YORK   PHILADELPHIA
MCMVI

Matchmaker or Romantic Hindrance?

How much did Anne Lefroy know about the abortive romance between Austen and her nephew, Jane's 'Irish friend', Tom Lefroy? He was staying with Anne when he met Jane and it's been claimed that she may have discouraged things getting serious between a couple who couldn't afford to marry. This story was denied by Anna, Jane's niece, who remembered that Madam Lefroy had turned against Tom because she thought he had 'behaved badly' to Jane. In 1797, another houseguest at Ashe, the Reverend Samuel Blackall, was introduced to Jane, and there are indications that Anne encouraged a possible match, sending him news of the Austens, and in particular of their younger daughter, after his departure. His reply, a triumph of obliqueness, put an end to any hopes: 'It would give me particular pleasure to have the opportunity of improving my acquaintance with that family', he wrote, 'with a hope of creating to myself a nearer interest. But at present I cannot indulge any expectation of it.' Again, the lack of funds may have been a problem.

A Sad Accident

Whether or not she had played matchmaker, Madam Lefroy and Jane Austen would remain close until Anne died in a fall from a skittish horse in 1804, on the same day that Jane turned 29. In 1808, Jane wrote a feeling poem in Anne's memory.

Below: A portrait of Anne Lefroy – painted by the miniaturist Richard Crosse in the 1770s, it neatly captures the intelligence and elegance so much admired by Jane Austen.

Opposite page: This edition of *Sense and Sensibility* has an engraving of Ashe Rectory, where George and Anne Lefroy lived with their family, on its title page.

'Angelic Woman! past my power to praise In Language meet, thy Talents, Temper, mind, Thy solid Worth, thy captivating Grace! – Thou friend & ornament of Humankind!'

—Jane Austen, extract from 'To the memory of Mrs Lefroy, who Died December 16 – My Birthday', 1808

A Burst of Creativity

A Quiet Home

Steventon became quieter after 1796; the Austen boys had all left home, and their parents finally closed the school which by then had been running successfully for over 20 years. With fewer distractions at home – and much less noise – it was probably no coincidence that the same year began an explosion in Jane's creativity.

Cassandra and Jane were now treated as adults by their parents. With more space in Steventon, they could have a 'day room' of their own – nothing grand, but the sisters could 'work' (sew), read or write in peace without interruptions. Jane's piano was kept there, as was the small lap desk that George Austen had given her as a nineteenth birthday present.

Elinor and Marianne

Dating specific parts of Austen's first three novels is difficult because they were not published until long after they'd been written, and all three were substantially revised on their path to publication. Much of what we know comes from Cassandra Austen's late-in-life recollections, and from occasional references in Jane's own letters. Jane started work on her first full-length novel, *Elinor and Marianne*, the book that would become *Sense and Sensibility*, in 1793 or 94. An early form of it was being

Right: 'Accomplishments' – in particular playing and singing – were much valued in young ladies in the late 18th and early 19th centuries.

Opposite top: Samuel Richardson's *Pamela*, published in 1740 and one of the most admired examples of the epistolary novel.

Opposite bottom: Goodnestone Manor House, yet another property of the Knight family, on the same estate as the smaller but still commodious Rowling, first home of Edward and Elizabeth Austen-Knight.

read aloud in the family circle by the following year, and there was a completed draft by 1796, even though this first version was in the same epistolary form as *Lady Susan* – that is, a novel made up of letters, harking back to Fielding's *Pamela* or Fanny Burney's *Evelina*. The form would change to a straight narrative long before the book was finally published.

A Visit to Kent

In the summer of 1796, Jane Austen spent some months on a visit to her brother Edward and his wife Elizabeth in Kent. From 1798 their base would be the much grander Godmersham, but their first married home was Rowling. Even at Rowling, the Austen-Knights had considerably more luxurious standards of living than Jane was accustomed to at Steventon, and she seems both to have enjoyed her comforts and to have chafed slightly at her inevitable status as a poor relation. She probably made a start on *First Impressions*, the book that would become *Pride and Prejudice*, on her return to Hampshire, and it was completed by the summer of 1797. Writing sharp portraits of rich, untroubled people like the Bingley sisters may have been a way to turn ruffled feelings into creative gold.

'Kent is the only place for happiness. Everybody is rich there.'

—Jane Austen, letter to Cassandra, 18 December 1798

Writing About Love

THE PRAGMATIC APPROACH
More than two centuries after their eventual publication, the status of Austen's novels is unchallengeable, but their modern categorisation as romantic novels is sometimes less sure. From today's perspective, the heroine always gets her man; from a Regency view, the picture was probably more complicated.

Taking Love Cautiously

In her mid-twenties, whatever her own romantic and marriage prospects, Jane Austen was surrounded by couples pairing off and marrying, sometimes for love, sometimes as more transactional alliances, often a mixture of both. The message the early novels send is one well established in her day – that it's wrong to marry for money, but stupid, or even impossible, to marry without it. The 'good' – prudent and well-behaved – Bennet sisters (Jane and Elizabeth) get love and money; the 'bad' sister (Lydia) ends up with neither. Charlotte Lucas makes an entirely transactional marriage – 'I am not romantic, you know. I never was. I ask only a comfortable home' – to the horror of her friend who cannot imagine being tied to Mr Collins. Over in *Sense and Sensibility*, Marianne Dashwood's highly 'sensible' and uncontrolled approach to love, aided and abetted by her equally emotional mother, gives her a false start in love; by the close of the novel – when she is still in her teens – she is

Right and opposite page: Unsuccessful proposals from Mr Darcy and Mr Collins in *Pride and Prejudice*, before Lizzy defends her acceptance of Darcy's second proposal to her father.

"You must allow me to tell you how ardently I admire and love you."

married off to a well-off older man who she 'esteems'; Elinor, with more common sense and a much less hysterical approach, has the husband she has loved from the start. Austen rewards good social behaviour in her novels but in real life she knows that love is only ever part of the equation. Mr Bennet, knowing nothing of Elizabeth's change of heart, is horrified when she proposes accepting Mr Darcy, however rich he may be, because he's worried about her being unhappy, as he is in his own marriage.

After Marriage

Austen's own later judgement of *Pride and Prejudice*, that it was 'rather too light, and bright, and sparkling; it wants shade' is probably what makes it supremely satisfying to the reader, who isn't required to care about any of the less well-behaved characters, but more shade does enter the later novels. Life, she well knew, is complicated. People once married were required to manage their income, to get along and to raise families.

'We all know him to be a proud, unpleasant sort of man; but this would be nothing if you really liked him.'

—Mr Bennet struggles to accept that Elizabeth is genuinely in love, *Pride and Prejudice*, 1813

'Love and eloquence.'

CHAPTER THREE

ADULTHOOD

Cassandra's Tragedy

SECRET ENGAGEMENT
Cassandra Austen had become engaged to Thomas Fowle in 1794. He was planning a career in the Church but the couple knew it might be a long time before they could marry; although he had been promised a family living it wasn't expected to become vacant for some years. In the meantime, the engagement was kept secret from all but close family members.

Tom still had to earn something. He took a job as a chaplain under the mentorship of his rich cousin, Lord Craven, and accompanied him on a voyage to the West Indies. Health-wise the tropics were known to be risky, but he must have thought the trip was worth it for the possible financial gain. He died of yellow fever in San Domingo early in 1797; ironically, Lord Craven later said that he would never have taken Tom with him if he had known of his engagement. Although the burial took place at sea on 13 February, news of his death didn't reach Cassandra, back in England, until April. She was said to have taken it calmly, but the effects of the loss were lifelong – at the age of 24, she turned her face against any future possibility of love or marriage.

Aftermath

As a bereaved fiancée, Cassandra did get recognition in Tom's will – he left her a bequest of £1,000, which gave her an annual income of around £50 – not a huge sum, but enough to give her a small amount of independence when planning visits, say, or buying clothes or books.

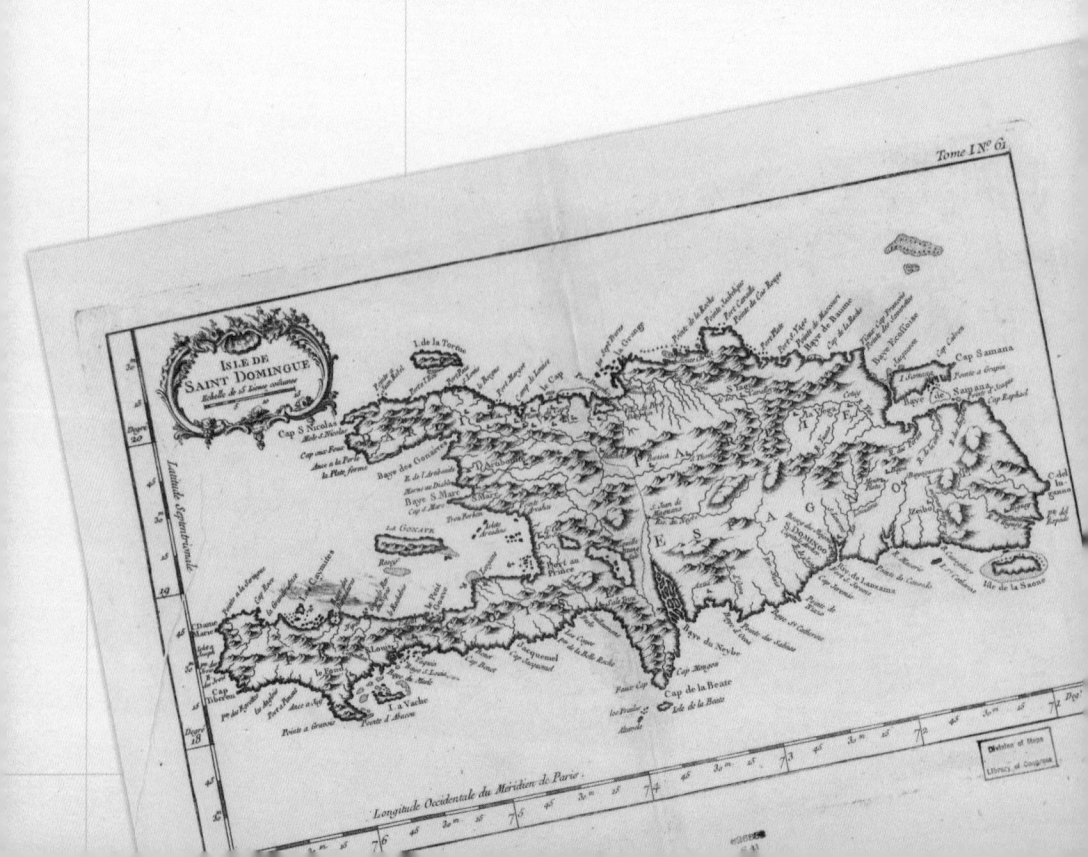

'... Alas instead of his arrival news were received of his Death... Jane says that her Sister behaves with a degree of resolution and Propriety which no common mind could evince in so trying a situation.'

—Letter from Eliza de Feuillide to Philadelphia Walter, 1797

Tom's death possibly had another result, this time for Cassandra's sister: relieved of any pressure Jane might have felt at the prospect of being the only unmarried Austen daughter, and guaranteed the continued close companionship of her sister, it may be that this was a point at which she reflected on whether she was likely to marry. Cassandra and Jane had always been inseparable – reflected in their mother's comment when Jane, aged just seven, insisted on accompanying her sister to school, that if Cassandra were going to have her head cut off, Jane would insist on sharing her fate. From this point, they seem to have become even closer.

Below: Ships headed to the West Indies in the 1790s were usually three-masted sloops like this one, HMS *Atalante* (although this example was built a few years later).

Opposite page: In the 1790s, the island of Santo Domingo (now Haiti and the Dominican Republic) was a French colony which had been destabilised by a major rebellion of enslaved people. By 1797 both British and Spanish forces were trying to exploit its instability. It has been estimated that about half the British on the campaign died of yellow fever – poor Tom Fowle was just one of its victims.

The First Approach

REJECTION
On 1 November 1797 George Austen wrote to the London publisher Cadell & Davies to ask if they would be able to consider a manuscript 'about the length of Miss Burney's *Evelina*' for publication. Cadell didn't bite – Austen's letter survives, with 'declined by Return of Post' written across the top. It would be another 14 years before *First Impressions*, by then renamed *Pride and Prejudice*, would find its reading public.

Cadell was a well-known and reputable publisher. His father, Thomas Cadell senior, had published titles by, among others, Samuel Johnson and the popular historian Edward Gibbon, and he had also been the first to bring the poems of Robert Burns to London.

On a less elevated note, he had been quick to follow the trend for romantic novels. Among many others, he had published *Cecilia*, by the already-established Fanny Burney, in 1782 and, in 1788, the incredibly successful *Emmeline: The Orphan of the Castle*, the first novel of the established poet Charlotte Smith. *Emmeline* was one of Jane Austen's own favourites and clearly plenty of other readers liked it, too: it ran through a sensational three editions in its first year of publication, a real triumph at a time when there were only a few reviews and books became popular largely by word of mouth.

Right: The older Thomas Cadell, who built a successful publishing company through his good instincts for popular novels as well as for more serious reading.

Opposite left: The multi-talented Charlotte Smith started her writing life as a poet, successfully branched into novels in the 1780s and would eventually become an author of popular children's books.

Opposite right: *The Italian*, the last novel Ann Radcliffe published in her lifetime, was a late success in the craze for melodramatic Gothic novels.

A Publishing Inheritance

On Cadell's retirement in 1793 his son, the second Thomas Cadell, succeeded him with his business partner, William Davies. The company remained successful. Although the rage for Gothic novels was beginning to wane by the late 1790s, in 1797, the year of George Austen's approach, Cadell had published *The Italian*, the final novel of Ann Radcliffe, the popular and well-respected mistress of Gothic suspense. He paid her £800, considered a very respectable sum.

Why didn't Cadell follow up with George Austen? Like publishers then and now, he was probably busy; the novel hadn't been included with the letter (in which case it might have had a chance of being picked up by a reader – even 18th-century publishers had slush piles) and Austen's tone was modest, citing neither literary connections nor a recommendation. What the letter tells us is that Austen's father knew that, at the age of 22, what she was writing would be enjoyed by a wider audience than her family and friends, and possibly commercially successful too.

> *'As I am well aware of what consequence it is that a work of this sort should make its first appearance under a respectable name, I apply to you.'*
>
> —George Austen tries a flattering tone on Thomas Cadell, 1 November 1797

Filling in the Gaps

'I am sure nobody can desire your letters as much as I do, and I don't think anyone deserves them so well.'

—Letter from Jane to Cassandra, written from Steventon, 25 November 1798

The part of Jane Austen's story that provokes the greatest dismay among scholars is the destruction of so many of her letters. Around 1842, long after Jane's death and just a year or two before her own, Cassandra went through their correspondence and destroyed or cut about most of Jane's letters to her, as well as disposing of any of hers to Jane. She didn't want the family's dirty laundry being washed in public. It's likely that Jane would have supported her – although acid extracts of some of those letters that do survive make one wonder how far Jane went in those that don't.

Turning Victorian

As Austen's posthumous success began to grow, a new generation started to take charge of her PR. The frank, pragmatic Georgian age was ending, the early Victorians were more shockable, and the younger Austens may have become keen to preserve the respectable image of their increasingly famous aunt. The result, though, was to leave some gaps in the story of the Austen sisters and Jane's development as a writer.

'... it is... most probable that our indifference will soon be mutual, unless his regard, which appeared to spring from knowing nothing of me at first, is best supported by never seeing me.'

—Letter from Jane to Cassandra, with a sardonic comment on Samuel Blackall's decreasing enthusiasm, 17 November 1798

Revealing Letters

We have twenty-odd letters between 1797 and the start of 1800. From a forest of hard-to-make-out gossip about family and friends, and calling on other surviving family records, we gather that Cassandra mourned stoically and carried on being helpful in her brothers' and sister-in-laws' lives, and that both James and Henry married in 1797. It was James's second marriage – to Mary Lloyd – while Henry was finally making a match with his beloved Eliza. We learn, too, that Edward and Elizabeth Austen-Knight carried on adding to their relentlessly growing family – their sixth child was born in 1800, and they would go on to have five more before childbearing finally killed Elizabeth.

Jane, back at her desk, found time between 1798 and 1799 to write the first draft of *Northanger Abbey* (this version called *Susan*) – giving her a completed, though unpublished, trio of novels at the start of the new century. A slightly painful passage in a letter from 1798 reveals that Madam Lefroy had told George Austen that Tom Lefroy had returned to Ireland to practise at the Bar there. This is the same letter in which Jane says that Mrs Lefroy has quoted Samuel Blackall as 'having no expectation' of pursuing a closer connection. For the moment at least, romantic possibilities seemed to be at an end.

Above: A late 19th-century illustration for *Northanger Abbey* – the novel is believed to be the first mature work completed by Jane Austen, although it was only published posthumously.

Opposite page: Queen Victoria acceded to the throne in 1837; the Jane described by her nephew, James Edward Austen-Leigh, in his 1869 memoir is seen through a demure Victorian lens, rather contradicted by Austen's own much less saccharine letters.

Upheaval

FAINTING FIT
One of the bits of history that every Austenite knows is that Jane was so shocked on being told the family was moving to Bath that she fainted dead away. This piece of family lore isn't really supported by contemporary accounts, but the news was certainly unwelcome – after all, she had been born at Steventon, as had Cassandra, and it was the only home they had ever known.

By 1800 George Austen was tired. He was nearly 70 and even after giving up the home school, maintaining the farm and parish interests at Steventon involved a lot of work. His oldest son James was living at Deane Rectory and was already acting as his father's curate, ready to take over Steventon when George retired. He and his wife may have looked forward to some well-earned leisure. Did he also wonder whether one or other of his daughters might finally find a husband in Bath? It's possible, and if Jane suspected it, it won't have made her any more positive about the move.

Bombshell News

Cassandra and Jane seem both to have been away on separate visits when the decision was taken, and they were told about it by their mother immediately on their return. There wasn't any lead-up or tactful breaking of the news, and there's a gap in Austen's letters between November 1800 and January 1801: any upset happens off-stage.

BATH.

THE PUMP ROOM, &c.

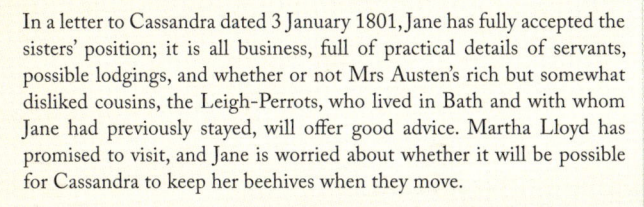

In a letter to Cassandra dated 3 January 1801, Jane has fully accepted the sisters' position; it is all business, full of practical details of servants, possible lodgings, and whether or not Mrs Austen's rich but somewhat disliked cousins, the Leigh-Perrots, who lived in Bath and with whom Jane had previously stayed, will offer good advice. Martha Lloyd has promised to visit, and Jane is worried about whether it will be possible for Cassandra to keep her beehives when they move.

Giving Things Up
George Austen held a house sale before their departure – 200 books from his treasured library appear in an auctioneer's notice in the *Reading Mercury* and *Oxford Gazette* on 20 May, along with 'neat household furniture', including the family's beds, all the 'kitchen dairy and brewing utensils' (sic), and Jane's pianoforte 'in a handsome case by Ganer'. James Austen bought most of his father's remaining books for what Jane felt was the knock-down price of just £70.

Above: Beekeeping was one of the rural pleasures that had to be given up when the Austen family decamped from Steventon to Bath.

Opposite page: Bath, although no longer the height of fashion by 1801, was still a very popular watering place. The handsome neo-classical Pump Room was so named because it housed the pumps which brought water from the hot springs for its clientele to drink.

'She disliked Bath, and did not think it agreed with her; and Bath was to be her home.'

—Anne Elliot, possibly echoing the feelings of Jane Austen about the family's move to Bath, *Persuasion*, 1817

Bath

HEALING WATERS
The Bath that the Austen family moved to in 1801 had been fashionable since the early 18th century and was no longer as exclusive as it had been. It was still a popular spa town, however, and it was hoped that taking the waters, and possibly other 'cures', would benefit Mrs Austen's much-discussed ill health.

Its showy new crescents and squares gave venerable Bath the look of a new town, but they were supported within the city by much less salubrious streets and terraces of workers' cottages. Finding appealing but affordable lodgings proved tricky: the Austens stayed a few weeks with the Leigh-Perrots at their smart home in Paragon Buildings before settling on 4 Sydney Place – a modern terrace with large windows, at a rent of £150 pa. It looked out onto Sydney Gardens, a modish small park, which had been prettily landscaped just a few years before.

Jane walked out with her uncle to take his second glass of spa water in the mornings, attended apparently endless social events – 'stupid parties' – entertained herself with bitchy remarks about other guests, and failed to make new friends, despite well-meaning and doubtless infuriating suggestions from her family. Then there's a silence: between May 1801 and September 1804, no more letters.

'Another stupid party last night; perhaps if larger they might be less intolerable... Miss Langley is like any other short girl, with a broad nose and wide mouth, fashionable dress and exposed bosom.'

—Letter from Jane, still staying with the Leigh-Perrots and not enjoying it, to Cassandra, 12 May 1801

COMFORTS of BATH.

An Absence of Inspiration

Even though she didn't think of it as home, Bath, as the background to most of *Northanger Abbey*, had already been useful to Jane's writing, but although she would set her last, wistful novel *Persuasion* there, it doesn't seem to have been immediately inspirational after the move.

In the absence of any first-person explanation, plenty of scholarly opinions are held as to why she seems to have almost stopped writing for several years. Although depression is often at the top of the list, another explanation may be that there was no opportunity. There was less space away from other people, there was a lot of virtually enforced socialising, and there was the care of her mother, who seems to have been seriously ill in 1801, shortly after the move. And, on top of the usual long visits to friends and relations, there was a new sort of travel: prolonged summer holidays to coastal resorts. Jane may not have liked Bath, but at least there were compensatory trips to the seaside.

Above: Early 18th-century view across Bath to Pulteney Bridge, taken from Spring Gardens, a popular pleasure ground. By 1800 this viewpoint had been obscured by some of the new houses that were going up all over the city.

Opposite page: A 1798 aquatint from the cartoonist Thomas Rowlandson's *Comforts of Bath* series, showing a raucous company taking breakfast together in one of the city's large public gathering rooms.

Travelling About

Beside the Seaside

For someone who had wanted to retire to Bath, George Austen didn't show much inclination to stay there after he arrived. Like a retiree today seized by an enthusiasm for cruises, he was disposed to travel – although in his case, it was trips into the West Country and to visit the seaside towns of Dorset and Devon.

If Bath sometimes felt socially claustrophobic to Jane, long holidays in rented accommodation in Sidmouth (in 1801), Dawlish, Teignmouth, and possibly Tenby (1802), Charmouth and Lyme Regis (1803) and Lyme Regis again (1804) supplied a much-needed change of scene.

Fresh Air and Freedom

The problems of not-very-salubrious lodgings never seem so difficult on holiday, and almost every mention of the seaside in Austen's writings is positive – free, airy, offering multiple possibilities. Poor Emma Woodhouse, limited in her travels by her father's imagined maladies, is jealous when the seaside is even mentioned; 'I must beg you not to talk of the sea. It makes me envious and miserable; I who have never seen it!' For Jane, sea bathing in particular was also a big success. It was a complicated business in the early 1800s – a wheeled bathing hut was pulled into the waves, usually by a donkey, then the bather emerged, and,

'A little sea-bathing would set me up forever.'

—Mrs Bennet yearns for the seaside, *Pride and Prejudice*, 1813

with the aid of a 'dipper', a strong helper hired along with the hut, was lowered into the sea, often remaining attached by a rope, to float about. To Jane Austen it must have represented a sensation of freedom that had been missed with the move to town and the absence of country walks.

A Holiday Affair?

There's an intriguing footnote to the coastal stays – in old age, Cassandra recalled to her nieces that on one holiday the sisters had met an extremely personable man who she believed had engaged Jane's affections and who had had feelings for her in return. He had promised to meet them on the following year's holiday, but shortly afterwards they heard that he had died. Much has been made of this since – frustratingly, though, exhaustive research hasn't succeeded in tying the story down. If Jane Austen did enjoy a seaside romance, perhaps it would be drawn upon for *Emma*, in which the secret engagement between eligible Frank Churchill and impoverished Jane Fairfax is entered into during a holiday at fashionable Weymouth.

> *'I continue quite well, in proof of which I have bathed again this morning. It was absolutely necessary that I should have the little fever and indisposition which I had; it has been all the fashion this week in Lyme.'*
>
> —Letter from Jane to Cassandra, 14 September 1804

Above: Two bathing huts, towed into place so that their occupants could be helped down their steps into the sea. The woman in the foreground has called for the services of two strong 'dippers' to support her as she wades in.

Opposite page and left: Seaside views of the beaches at Charmouth and Sidmouth as Austen would have seen them.

The Proposal

A Promising Offer
As far as we know, Jane received one certain proposal of marriage. It may not have been as romantic as Cassandra's story of summer romance, but it was accompanied by the promise of both a fortune and property, and it must have been tempting as she accepted it briefly before changing her mind the following day.

Told by family members at several removes, the facts seem to be these. In 1802, at the end of that year's seaside holiday, Jane and Cassandra went on, first to stay at Steventon, then to Manydown for a visit with Alethea and Catherine Bigg. After staying there a week, the Biggs' younger brother, 21-year-old Harris Bigg-Wither (men of the family took a hyphenated surname, while the ladies remained plain Bigg), proposed to Jane Austen, and she accepted him.

A Change of Heart

The next morning she told him that she had changed her mind, making it too embarrassing for the Austens to stay any longer. Alethea and Catherine, probably confused and upset themselves, ordered their carriage to take Jane and Cassandra back to Steventon. The sisters usually deferred to the convenience of their older brother, but this time they insisted that James take them back to Bath immediately.

Why did she accept? And why did she then refuse? She probably accepted because she was already fond of his family, and she at least 'esteemed' Harris, having known him since he was a boy. He is described as having awkward manners, but he was also heir to a large fortune and, eventually, to Manydown, a house where she had had many happy visits. Thinking it through overnight, she probably pondered the other inevitabilities: forced intimacy where there wasn't love, and the inevitable prospect of childbirth, perilous and, in the early 19th century, not infrequently fatal. And, as a married woman, it would be unlikely that she would have any time for writing. She wasn't mercenary enough to see it through.

Left: The moment of the proposal is always one of high tension in Austen's novels, although her own experience doesn't seem to have been a romantic one.

'What did she say? Just what she ought, of course. A lady always does. She said enough to show there need not be despair – and to invite him to say more himself.'

—Emma Woodhouse, managing Mr Knightley's proposal more smoothly, *Emma*, 1815

In a letter telling the whole story, sent in 1870, Caroline, daughter of James Austen, was forgiving of her loved aunt: 'To be sure, she should not have said "Yes" overnight; but I have always respected her for her courage in cancelling that "Yes" the next morning; all worldly advantages would have been to her, and she was of an age to know this quite well (she was nearly twenty-seven).'

Pattens and Caps

SIGNS OF AGEING
Family members remembered Jane and Cassandra taking on the trappings of older women while they were still in their twenties: there are mentions of their nieces carping about their habit of wearing caps in the evening while other ladies of similar age were still dressing their hair attractively. Caps – the making, trimming and wearing of them – certainly get plenty of mentions in Jane's letters.

We can't really tell how much the Austen sisters worried about personal style from Jane's letters, although they talk a good deal about clothes. In her letters, most of Jane's references to what she wears are humorous or practical – the concerns are always to be neat and respectable – but like all Regency women of even modest means, she had to take some interest because her clothes were made from scratch. You might take inspiration from engravings in publications like *The Gallery of Fashion*, or you might copy a friend whose clothes you liked, but how you dressed, in an age before ready-made, was very much up to you, and involved several processes, from choosing the style of dress to buying the fabric and commissioning the mantua-maker (dressmaker) to cut and sew it.

'I have made myself two or three caps to wear of evenings since I came home, and they save me a world of torment as to hair-dressing...'

—Letter from Jane, unembarrassed about her headgear, to Cassandra, 1 December 1798

A Dangerous Age

Their nieces' memories were faintly mocking of their prematurely aged style – we are left with a picture of Jane and Cassandra, dressed alike, walking out of doors, wearing the old-fashioned wooden overshoes, or pattens, which protected shoes from muddy lanes, or, in the evenings, donning caps to save the trouble of hairdressing. The result is a picture of confirmed, perhaps contented, spinsters when they were still only in their late twenties.

Twenty-seven seems to have been a pivotal age both for Austen herself and for her heroines. In *Persuasion*, Anne Elliot has lost her bloom early; having been a very pretty girl at 19, only eight years later her past suitor Captain Wentworth declares he would hardly have known her. In *Sense and Sensibility*, lovely, immature 17-year-old Marianne Dashwood is even blunter: 'A woman of seven and twenty,' she declares, 'can never hope to feel or inspire affection again.' At 27, *Pride and Prejudice*'s Charlotte Lucas opts for an unenviable bridegroom rather than embracing spinsterhood.

If being unmarried at 27 years old was potentially a dangerous descent into old-maidism, Jane reached it shortly after refusing Harris Bigg-Wither, and, along with Cassandra, it seems to have been the point at which she set her style and, to some extent, decided her future.

Right: Fashionable walking dresses of 1808. The cap on the right has a drooping fabric brim to shade its wearer's face; by definition caps were softer and less formal than bonnets, which were stiffened or woven into more structured shapes.

Opposite page: An image of Jane, based on a small drawing by Cassandra, but painted – and glamorised – in the last quarter of the 19th century. It shows the way in which short curls of hair were pulled out from under the cap to frame the face.

A Second Approach

REVISIONS

Refusing an offer of marriage may have sent Jane back to her manuscripts. We know she made plenty of revisions to her 'finished' early books, but early in 1803 she decided that *Susan* (eventually published as *Northanger Abbey*) was ready to be offered to a publisher. Set in Bath and with a plot that revolved around Gothic novels, it may have seemed the most topical of her completed books.

The First Sale

Presumably she discussed it with the family, and Henry, the brother she was closest to, probably helped with the choice of publisher – Benjamin Crosby, while based in London, had a wide network of connections, including one with a Bath bookseller called Cruttwell. Enquiry at the latter may have led to a recommendation for the former. Crosby was a prolific publisher of novels, including many Gothic titles; the actual negotiations over the purchase of *Susan* were made by Henry's lawyer, William Seymour, and resulted in Crosby buying the copyright of the novel outright for £10 – not generous, but not a scandalously low offer for an unknown author.

Dashed Hopes

Crosby advertised *Susan* as part of his forthcoming list that summer (other titles included the intriguing-sounding *Monteville Castle: The Depraved Husband and the Philosophic Wife*, which would surely have come high on Catherine Morland's reading list) but the book failed to appear. The mystery as to why he bought a book he didn't publish may have been solved by recent research that suggests he had money

'This little work was finished in the year 1803, and intended for immediate publication. It was disposed of to a bookseller, it was even advertised, and why the business went no farther, the author has never been able to learn.'

—Jane's note accompanying the advertisement for the eventual publication of *Northanger Abbey*, 1817

troubles – he hadn't paid much, but printing was expensive, so if he published it and it failed to do well, he would have been sending good money after bad.

It must have been a blow to Austen, however, as a yet-to-be-published author, when subsequent years ticked by and the book didn't appear. We only hear of *Susan* again when she wrote directly to Crosby in April 1809, nearly six years later, acknowledging her authorship but under an assumed name, Mrs Ashton Dennis – signature MAD – to ask why he hadn't published it and threatening to publish it herself. His equally irritable reply told her that if she could repay the £10, she was welcome to it; otherwise, it remained his property. With no money of her own, she presumably felt stuck: the rights wouldn't be retrieved until 1815, and the renamed book would only – finally – be published shortly after its author's death.

Below: Jane would revise and update the book when it was eventually bought back from Crosby, but also wrote a note for readers explaining why it might feel like a period piece.

Opposite page: *Northanger Abbey*'s long journey to publication took 14 years; having accepted – and even advertised it, under its original title of *Susan* – Benjamin Crosby then failed to publish the novel.

ADVERTISEMENT

By the Authoress

of

NORTHANGER ABBEY.

This little work was finished in the year 1803, and intended for immediate publication. It was disposed of to a bookseller, it was even advertised, and why the business proceeded no farther, the author has never been able to learn. That any bookseller should think it worth while to purchase what he did not think it worth while to publish, seems extraordinary. But with this, neither the author nor the public have any other concern than as some observation is necessary upon those parts of the work which thirteen years have made comparatively obsolete. The public are entreated to bear in mind that thirteen years have passed since it was finished, many more since it was begun, and that during that period, places, manners, books, and opinions have undergone considerable changes.

A New Work

THE WATSONS

Perhaps fuelled by the acceptance of *Susan*, at some point late in 1803 or early in 1804, Jane began work on a brand-new novel. It was never to be finished; today the fragment that we have left is known as *The Watsons*. It would finally be published in 1871, by which time anything written by Austen was becoming interesting to an ever-growing number of enthusiasts.

James Edward Austen-Leigh, responsible for the eventual publication, put forward the idea that Austen had stopped work on it because she had mistakenly set her central characters too low on the social scale and found it hard to continue – a particularly odd argument, as the position of the family in the plot – the four unmarried daughters of an impoverished clergyman, one of whom has been brought up and educated by richer relatives – was in every regard one with which Jane would have been very familiar.

Even the tantalisingly small piece of *The Watsons* we have is an enjoyable read with a heroine who, pretty, lively and unaffected, is somewhat reminiscent of Elizabeth Bennet, but who is in a far more precarious situation. The manuscript itself is also interesting because it shows us Jane working on something new: heavily scored and overwritten, it is raw material, quite different from the fine copies she made of her novels when she considered them complete.

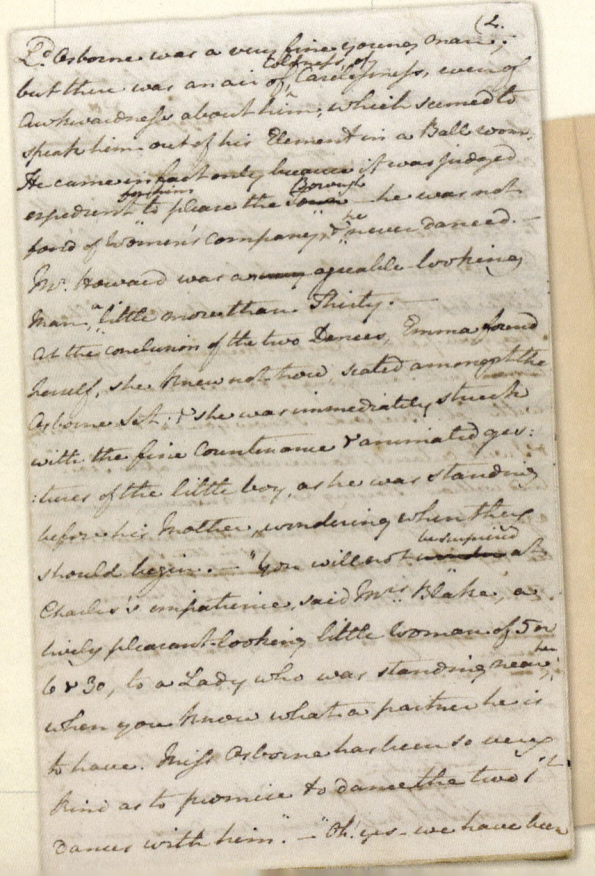

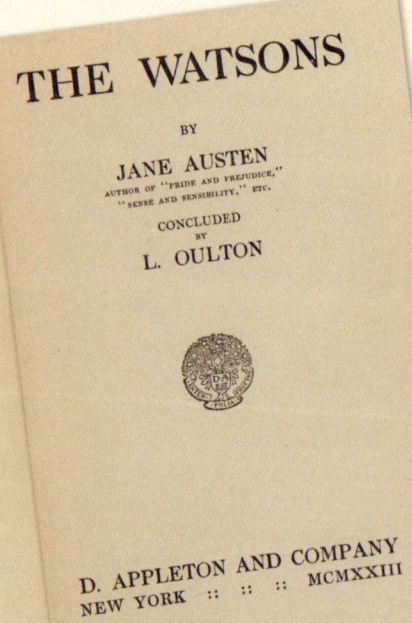

> *'Poverty is a great evil, but to a woman of education and feeling it ought not, it cannot be the greatest. I would rather be a teacher at a school (and I can think of nothing worse) than marry a man I did not like.'*
>
> —Emma Watson remains idealistic about marriage, *The Watsons*, 1871

Another Move

In 1804, three years into life in Bath, the lease on Sydney Place came up, and when the Austens returned from their holiday – that year, at Lyme Regis – they moved to a slightly less genteel address – the newly built Green Park Buildings East. The reason for moving was probably financial; George Austen was having difficulty making ends meet. The new accommodation was perfectly acceptable, although the houses were located on the flood plain of the River Avon and therefore tended to be damp, a problem that the family had become quite used to at Steventon, but which wasn't good for either George or Mrs Austen's health. Nonetheless, they seemed to settle in comfortably enough. Events soon after the move, though, were enough reason for Jane to lay *The Watsons* aside, apparently for good.

Above: 4 Sydney Place, the Austens' first rented home in Bath, photographed around 1920.

Opposite page: *The Watsons* is one of few Austen manuscripts to have survived at draft stage, although even its crossings-out are characteristically neat.

The Death of Mr Austen

SUDDEN DEATH
George Austen died suddenly after a very short illness. Mrs Austen had been seriously ill in 1804, but had recovered; in contrast, her husband's illness didn't seem worrying at first. On 19 January 1805 he complained of a headache and a fever; he improved briefly after he had been visited by a surgeon and 'cupped' – still a common treatment in the early 1800s – but took a turn for the worse over the following night. He died shortly after 10 o'clock on the morning of Monday, 21 January.

Researchers today believe that the most likely cause of death was sepsis. In the days before antibiotics, it's unlikely that anything a doctor could have done would have saved him. As seems to have been the Austen family's habit, they took the disaster stoically. Their grieving was undisrupted by any Mrs Bennet-style hysterics; letters speak of the comfort they took in their religion and the Reverend George's virtuous and godly life. 'The Serenity of the Corpse is most delightful!' wrote Jane to her brother Francis, who was serving on HMS *Leopard* in Portsmouth, 'It preserves the sweet, benevolent smile which always distinguished him.'

Right: Cupping: the glass was heated, applied to the patient's skin, then removed. A surgeon might then make small incisions in the cupped area and bleed the patient of excess fluid.

FROM PARK PLACE.

All Change

It had been a dreadful few weeks. Jane was still in shock from the news of another unexpected death – that of her friend, Madam Lefroy, on 16 December 1804, after a fall from her horse. The loss of her father, though, went far beyond an emotional blow – it also transformed his widow's and daughters' economic circumstances overnight. He had continued to draw the income from the livings of Steventon and Deane, paying James as their curate, but now he was dead, his income immediately died with him.

The lease on Green Park Buildings was paid up until the end of March, so at least they had a roof over their heads. Cassandra had the small allowance from the money left her by Tom Fowle, and Mrs Austen had a slightly larger annual amount from personal family investments. Pooled, this probably added up to around £200 a year – far less than would keep the household in the modest but comfortable style to which they were accustomed.

Above: At Mr Austen's death there were only three months' lease remaining on the Austens' lodgings at Green Park Buildings (the houses seen here in the foreground, looking on to the River Avon).

'Our dear Father has closed his virtuous & happy life, in a death almost as free from suffering as his Children could have wished... The loss of such a Parent must be felt, or we should be Brutes.'

—Letter from Jane to Francis Austen, 21 January 1805

Nomads

THE AUSTEN BROTHERS
With Mr Austen gone, and the sisters and their mother reliant on a very small income indeed, it fell to the Austen sons to look after them. Everyone seems to have behaved quite characteristically, perhaps without much enquiry as to what circumstances Mrs Austen, Cassandra and Jane themselves might prefer.

Gathering an Income

First, money. Edward, by far the richest of the family, said he would contribute £100 per year. Given that an estimate of his annual income at the time was £15,000, one might feel that this was the least he could have done. James and Henry each offered £50 per year, and Francis, who was doing well in his naval career, offered to give £100 per year but was knocked back to £50 by Mrs Austen who feared he was being too generous. Charles, youngest in the family and living on a ship far away in Bermuda, doesn't seem to have chipped in. With the contributions, the Austen women's income had been built back up to around £450 per year.

A Place to Live

Mrs Austen laid off two of her three servants and in March 1805 she and her daughters moved to 25 Gay Street, another step down the Bath ladder. January 1806 saw another move, this time to lodgings in Trim Street – a street of old and poky houses which represented the nadir of their time in Bath. Luckily their stay there would last only six months – in July 1806 the Austen ladies left the town for the final time. This time they were accompanied by Martha Lloyd, on her own since her mother had died, and, with such strong ties of friendship with the Austen sisters, about to join their household for good.

They left at Frank Austen's suggestion. He had fought in the Battle of San Domingo, and the prize money he'd been awarded had enabled him to marry. His new wife, Mary, would be alone while he was at sea, and he felt it would make sense for his mother, sisters and Martha to pool resources and share a household with her in Southampton. Eventually all five moved into a house with a large garden at Castle Square, overlooking the sea. They liked it at first, although living communally with Mary doesn't seem to have worked out in the long term; in any case, the constant round of visits and family duties carried on, so they weren't usually there for long periods. Nonetheless, they stayed until the family made their final move to Chawton Cottage.

Above: If they won a naval battle, British sailors were given prize money – a portion of the proceeds from any ships captured and subsequently sold. The prize money he was awarded after the Battle of San Domingo, 1806, shown here, considerably enriched Frank Austen.

Opposite page: Gay Street, the much pokier lodgings the Austen women moved to – briefly – in 1805.

'Could my Ideas flow as fast as the rain in the Storecloset, it would be charming... the contest between us & the Closet has now ended in our defeat...'

—Letter from Jane, bemoaning the difficulties of living in an old, leaky house, to Cassandra, 24 January 1809

Chapter Four

Chawton

Family Events

Disputed Will

The years before Mrs Austen and her daughters settled at Chawton were eventful in the wider family. Two events were particularly notable; the first was the saga of a huge family legacy, disputed by cousins who were (in Jane's view at least) already quite rich enough.

In August 1806, on one of their customary visits to Mrs Austen's elderly cousin, the Reverend Francis Leigh, at Adlestrop, he suggested the Austen ladies accompany him to stay at Stoneleigh Abbey in Warwickshire, home of his recently deceased cousin, the Honourable Mary Leigh. Due to one of those vague wills that invariably cause trouble, Mary's estate fell due to Francis – but seemed to give the Leigh-Perrots, Mrs Austen's wealthy Bath cousins, an (almost) equal claim to it.

Below: Stoneleigh Abbey, in Warwickshire, owned by the Leigh family from the 16th century and probably the grandest house Austen ever stayed in.

STONELEIGH ABBEY.
THE RESIDENCE OF CHANDOS LEIGH ESQ⟨?⟩

Disappointed Expectations

Stoneleigh Abbey was an immense mansion, and the Austens stayed for a fortnight, amazed by the grandeur of their surroundings. Behind the scenes, negotiations were going on to sort out the inheritance. The Leigh-Perrots agreed to give up their claim if the Reverend Thomas paid them a lump sum of £20,000 plus an income of £2,000 a year for life. Thomas Leigh and his lawyers suggested that some part of this sum should be settled on poorer members of the family. Briefly it seemed the Austen ladies might benefit. Expectations rose high, but sadly came to nothing: rich though both parties involved were, they were not feeling generous. The slightly disorderly glamour of Stoneleigh may have been borrowed for some of the great houses in Jane's novels, but ultimately that – and a small direct bequest, of a diamond ring, from the Honourable Mary – would be the only joy she would have of it.

A Family Tragedy

The loss of a potential legacy must have been a disappointment, but October 1808 brought a calamity for Edward Austen and his children: Elizabeth, his poised, beautiful wife, died suddenly at Godmersham, shortly after giving birth to their eleventh child. Cassandra had already been helping to run things during Elizabeth's confinement; she stayed on for some months. Edward was lost without his well-loved wife, and the children were devastated. Young Edward and George, two of the teenage sons, stayed with Jane for a while at Southampton, where she made valiant attempts to entertain and distract them.

'We have felt, we do feel for you all – as you will not need to be told – for you, for Fanny, for Henry, for Lady Bridges, & for dearest Edward, whose loss & whose sufferings seem to make those of every other person nothing.'

—Letter from Jane to Cassandra, 13 October 1808

A House of Their Own

EDWARD'S OFFER
It's not known why Edward Austen, with plenty of property, took so long to offer his mother and sisters somewhere permanent to live. In 1806 Frank's suggestion of a house share in Southampton may have come up before his older brother thought of it. When Southampton showed signs of not working out as well as hoped, however, the newly widowed Edward made them an offer.

Mrs Austen and her daughters were given two options for houses that might suit them. One was in Rye, the village nearest to Godmersham – but the one the ladies chose was Chawton Cottage. Despite its name, today it would be considered a fair-sized house, with six bedrooms. It was built of brick, well over a century old, and had been at different times in the past a farmhouse and an inn; most recently, it had been the home of Edward's land agent. Edward took some trouble to do it up ready for its new occupants – records show he spent about £80 on building, redecoration and plumbing.

Outside, Chawton had a decent-sized plot, with a small orchard, a pond, space to grow flowers and vegetables, and the gravel 'walk' that seems to have been indispensable to gardens at that date, although it was also located beside a busy – by early 19th-century standards – road. Chawton House, another of Edward's grand homes, was nearby, and Steventon was not far away.

Settling In

The Austens left Castle Square for the final time in May and, after a round of visits, moved into Chawton early in July 1809, accompanied by Martha Lloyd, now a permanent member of the household. There's one of those infuriating gaps in Jane's letters between that summer and the spring of 1811; the only personal view we have is in a poem that she wrote on 26 July. She composed it to congratulate Frank Austen on the birth of a son, but it goes on:

> 'As for ourselves, we're very well,
> As unaffected prose will tell.
> Cassandra's pen will give our state
> The many comforts that await
> Our Chawton home – how much we find
> Already in it to our mind,
> And how convinced that when complete,
> It will all other Houses beat...'

The cheerful couplets sound as though the Austens were happily engaged in arranging things to their taste, without the worry of lease, landlord or – presumably – the leaks that had been such a feature of Castle Square whenever there was heavy rain.

Opposite page: Chawton House, here seen in the distance, was just a stroll across the park from Chawton Cottage.

Above: This early photograph has been identified as a portrait of Martha Lloyd in old age, pet terrier on knee. Long after Jane's death, at the age of 62, she became Frank Austen's second wife, cementing her lifelong connection with the family.

Domestic Matters

MODERN-DAY MUSEUM
Today it's the Jane Austen House Museum, and Chawton Cottage remains the place where Austenites can most easily place Jane in their imaginations, whether visiting in person or looking at photographs.

The family seem to have settled in quickly to a routine. Mrs Austen enjoyed sitting in the dining room in the mornings, looking out onto the main road and watching who went past. The drawing room had a quieter outlook – the window had been moved from the front to the side, so that it looked over greenery, and Jane played the piano there in the early mornings. Afterwards she prepared breakfast; Cassandra and Martha were in charge of the other meals and most of the day-to-day housekeeping, and Mrs Austen, now in her seventies, liked to look after the garden. 'In charge' would have largely meant managing the staff – the grim days of Trim Street with a single maid were long over: the four-woman household was back up to a full complement of two maids, a cook and a manservant.

Below: Chawton Cottage, seen from the road. To the left of the door you can see where a window facing the street has been blocked off – the new window around the corner ensured the second front room had a much quieter outlook.

Chawton House

If this description leaves the impression of a quiet, rather confined life, it leaves out the Austens' visiting habits. Having finally found a safe berth, Mrs Austen tended to stay at home, but Jane, Cassandra and Martha were all still often away on visits and family visited them: the nieces and nephews came to stay, and sometimes their brothers' whole households descended on them. Chawton House, a 16th-century mansion set in a large park, another part of the Knights' estate, was just a 10-minute walk away, although it was let to tenants until 1812 when Edward's adoptive mother Mrs Knight died in Canterbury. He and his family had lived mainly at Godmersham to be close to her; now they spent far more time in Hampshire, taking up residence at Chawton House. With James still at Steventon, the area was now thick with Austens and Knights.

'The Chicken are all alive, & fit for the Table – but we save them for something grand. Some of the Flower seeds are coming up very well – but your Mignonette makes a wretched appearance… the whole of the Shrubbery Border will soon be very gay with Pinks & Sweet Williams, in addition to the Columbines already in bloom.'

— Letter from Jane to Cassandra, filling her in on domestic details, 29 May 1811

Back to Writing

Working From Home

Decades after her death a mythology had sprung up around Jane's writing habits at Chawton, fed by James Edward Austen-Leigh's 1869 memoir. She wrote in secret, his story went, laying the pages aside if she heard a step in the passage '… careful that her occupation should not be suspected by servants, or visitors, or any persons beyond her own family party.' A creaking swing door gave enough warning for her to put her work away if anyone arrived. We know that she wrote in miniature notebooks folded from sheets of larger paper; according to Austen-Leigh this was so that they could be easily concealed.

Below: The parlour at Chawton where Jane Austen wrote. Her folding writing desk is shown, open, on top of the table.

Did she really go to such lengths to keep her work secret? The memoir describes a sort of domestic-goddess Jane, very unlike the acerbic presence we feel in the letters – a natural genius, modestly intent on keeping her light under a bushel. But the newly composed household at Chawton seems deliberately to have freed some time to allow her to get on with her work, and all her novels were extensively discussed and read among her intimates while they were still works in progress – Jane joked that Martha read *First Impressions* so many times that she could steal it and reproduce it as her own.

It's perfectly believable, though, that she didn't want to talk writing with anyone she didn't know well, and even after she became successful, she was always nervous of playing the part of star author. 'We neither of us perform to strangers', says Darcy to Elizabeth in *Pride and Prejudice*, and he may have been speaking of his creator, too.

After Jane's death, Cassandra wrote and initialled a note of the dates she remembered the books had been written – it goes:

TIME TO WRITE

There are indications that Jane went back to more regular writing very soon after the move to Chawton. Her domestic role seems to have been limited to making the breakfast and taking charge of the supplies of wine, tea and sugar that comprised the household's small luxuries. She paid visits and had visitors, she still did her own sewing – both plain and fancy – but she also had time to dedicate to her work.

First Impressions begun in Oct. 1796 Finished in Augt 1797 – Published afterwards, with alterations & contractions under the Title of Pride & Prejudice.

Sense & Sensibility begun Nov. 1797. I am sure that something of the same story & characters had been written earlier & called Elinor & Marianne.

Mansfield Park, begun somewhere about Feby 1811 – Finished soon after June 1813

Emma begun Jany 21st 1814, finished March 29th 1815.

Persuasion begun Augt 8th 1815 Finished Augt 6th 1816

North-hanger Abbey was written about the years 98 & 99

C.E.A.

Reading Habits

Keen Reader
While Austen got back down to writing – correcting her earlier manuscripts and introducing revisions and updates where they were necessary – she remained an avid reader. As usual, books were loaned from friends or libraries, keenly discussed and carefully noted: for a long time she had been reading not just as a consumer, but with an eye to her own writing.

We know Jane was a regular reader of history, and travel works; sermons and other religious books; plus some works in French, including those of Madame de Staël, but her reading continued to include plentiful novels. Her lifetime was a heyday for novels written by women, so there were always works by lady novelists with whom she could compare herself directly.

Other People's Novels
The literary lioness of Austen's time was Maria Edgeworth – Anglo-Irish with excellent connections and an intellectual edge, she was successful and prolific, with smartly plotted novels about society. Today they seem far less innovative than Austen's own, but as late as 1869 Austen-Leigh's memoir commented that outsiders would have found the view of Jane's family – that her novels were the equals of Miss Edgeworth's wildly popular books – extraordinary. Jane herself was dazzled by her. 'I have made up my mind to like no Novels really, but Miss Edgeworth's, Yours & my own', she would write to her niece, Anna, who was trying her own hand at writing a novel, in 1813.

Clever Writing

Jane comments on what other people are writing like a professional. When, in 1811, she tells Cassandra that she has been trying to get hold of the popular new bestseller, *Self-Control*, by the now-forgotten Mary Brunton, she also admits that she always worries, as she opens a 'clever' novel, that she will find her own ideas in it, but somehow used more successfully. When it came to *Self-Control*, she needn't have worried – Laura, its pious heroine, undergoes many unlikely ordeals, the highlight being an abduction to America, ending with a trip down raging river rapids while lashed to a canoe. All of which amused Jane, when she finally got her hands on a copy.

'I am looking over Self Control again, & my opinion is confirmed of its being an excellently-meant, elegantly-written Work, without anything of Nature or Probability in it. I declare I do not know whether Laura's passage down the American River, is not the most natural, possible, every-day thing she ever does.'

—Letter from Jane to Cassandra, 11 October 1813

Left: Mary Brunton, Scottish novelist. Her own life was adventurous – born on Orkney, she eloped by rowing boat to become the wife of Alexander Brunton – both Professor of Oriental Languages at Edinburgh University and Minister of Edinburgh's Greyfriars Kirk. As well as *Self-Control*, she published *Discipline* in 1815, and *Emmeline* in 1819.

Opposite page: Maria Edgeworth lived a long life, unmarried but surrounded by her large family in County Longford, Ireland. She and Austen had a mutual admiration, although Edgeworth did criticise *Emma* for being – in her view – dismally uneventful. She died in 1849, having outlived Jane by more than three decades.

Life at the Great House

OBSERVANT VISITOR
Jane Austen's realistic depictions of vicarage life were based on her direct experience. Her grander houses, however – Pemberley, Mansfield and Sotherton, among others – were drawn from a lifetime of visiting, and she would never enter them on quite equal terms.

Below: Screen adaptations of Jane's novels call for vision on the part of location scouts to match the fictional mansions with real ones. The much-loved 2005 TV production of *Pride and Prejudice* used Palladian Basildon Park to play the part of Netherfield.

All Austen's novels contain houses of standing. *Sense and Sensibility* opens with the Dashwood women being exiled from consequential Norland Park; in *Pride and Prejudice*, there's Pemberley, in which Elizabeth is first a day tripper before becoming its mistress. Emma Woodhouse has Hartfield (and will probably end up at Donwell Abbey), while Northanger Abbey and Mansfield Park actually take the titles of their books. The final novel, *Persuasion* has another exiled heroine: Anne Elliot has to leave Kellynch Hall because of the extravagance of her vain father, who has frittered away his fortune.

The Real Thing

Over time, Austen would gather material – she spent time in plenty of consequential houses. There was comfortable, commodious Manydown of which she briefly had the chance of being mistress, and her brother Edward's country estates, the even-grander Godmersham and Chawton House. There was also her odd, one-off visit to the splendours of Stoneleigh Abbey.

Inevitably, visits were in the role of a poor relation; she and Cassandra were constantly on call, sometimes to make themselves useful with their brothers' children or, on occasion, their sick or confined wives. Perhaps tellingly, the most enduring friendship Jane made at Godmersham was with Anne Sharp, who was, for a couple of years, governess to her niece Fanny.

Into Literature

In her novels, large houses were used quite subtly; contemporary readers would have been able to distinguish easily between new and old money. Bingley's fortune comes through industry, for example; he has no family 'seat' – Netherfield is rented – while Darcy, who is old money, has Pemberley, an ancestral pile with plenty of land. The Bertrams of grand, modern Mansfield Park are new money, too – Sir Thomas's fortune is from plantations in Antigua – while Mr Rushworth, unappealing fiancé of Maria Bertram, has a main, some might say sole, asset: Sotherton, a huge, Tudor brick mansion, home to his family for generations.

By the time she wrote *Mansfield Park*, Jane had enough experience to write confidently about what living in such houses – with their butlers, governesses and dozens of anonymous servants – would be like.

Below and below left: In the 2004 Ang Lee-directed movie of *Sense and Sensibility*, Montacute House, an Elizabethan mansion in Somerset, stood in – rather grandly – for Cleveland, the country home of the Palmers. Montacute's Great Chamber is shown below and its main front, below left.

'And of this place', thought she, 'I might have been mistress!'

—Elizabeth Bennet is dazzled by Pemberley, *Pride and Prejudice*, 1813

Austen's Landscape

A Country Village
Jane's well-worn comment from an 1814 letter to Anna Austen, that '3 or 4 Families in a Country Village is the very thing [for the novelist] to work on', leaves out the countryside around them, but there's plenty of evidence that rural surroundings were important to her.

Below: *A View of Boxhill from Norbury Park, Surrey*, painted in around 1775 by the artist Thomas Sandford.

Opposite page: 'Engaged by the River' – an illustration showing Mr Darcy and Mr Gardiner fishing together at Pemberley, from an 1894 edition of *Pride and Prejudice*.

Although detailed descriptions of landscapes are rare in her novels, when they do appear, they're heartfelt. In Bath, she and Cassandra had had only the pretty, tailored little landscape of Sydney Gardens to enjoy; back in Hampshire, when the weather allowed, there was plenty of walkable country, including the large park of Chawton House. Elizabeth Bennet is sarcastically praised by the Bingley sisters – who probably prefer to see the countryside from a carriage – as 'an excellent walker', and so was Jane. Sometimes, too, the landscape is a revelation – Elizabeth jokingly attributes her love for Darcy as having started when she saw the beauties of his estate at Pemberley.

Particularly in the later novels, Austen occasionally writes about landscape apparently just for the love of it. *Persuasion* has such a passage describing Charmouth, 'a scene so wonderful and so lovely', and there's another in *Emma*: the strawberry-picking outing to Mr Knightley's house, Donwell Abbey, gives rise to one of Austen's best descriptions. It's lovely writing in itself, but Austen is also using it to 'sell' the reader a specifically English setting in a way that would appeal to people much better travelled than her, and familiar with a far greater variety of landscapes.

Romantic Landscape

Austen places the reader in front of a panorama of the scene, then sweeps across it: 'The considerable slope, at nearly the foot of which the Abbey stood, gradually acquired a steeper form beyond its grounds; and at half a mile distant was a bank of considerable abruptness and grandeur, well clothed with wood; and at the bottom of this bank, favourably placed and sheltered, rose the Abbey-Mill Farm, with meadows in front, and the river making a close and handsome curve around it...

'... It was a sweet view – sweet to the eye and the mind. English verdure, English culture, English comfort, seen under a sun bright, without being oppressive.'

—*Emma*, 1815

Nieces and Nephews

BELOVED AUNT
In many ways Jane Austen seemed born to be an aunt – which was lucky, as her brothers fathered 33 children with multiple wives. Later, many of the younger generation would remember her holding an important place in their childhood.

Jane could invent games with gusto, stage plays and read stories. She was quick to empathise, too. When her teenage nieces were older, she could discuss matters of the heart both sensibly and sensitively. This didn't mean that she wasn't sharply critical of nephews and nieces when they irritated her, although negative opinions seem mostly to have been expressed about rather than to them.

Cassandra was loved too, but never seems to have raised quite as much enthusiasm among her young relatives as her sister – perhaps she was a more stolid character. She tended to be the one called in to help when her brothers' wives were having babies, but was less applauded for her imagination and energy once the children were older.

Right: Fanny Knight hard at work with her watercolours, like every accomplished young lady, painted by her aunt, Cassandra Austen. Fanny notes 'Aunt Cassandra took my likeness' in her diary on 3 September 1805, when she would have been 12 years old.

'Now that you are become an Aunt, you are a person of some consequence & must excite great Interest whatever You do. I have always maintained the importance of Aunts as much as possible, & I am sure of your doing the same now.'

—Letter from Jane to her niece Caroline, whose sister, Anna Lefroy, had just had her first baby, 30 October 1815

Key Nieces

Two of her nieces stand out as having been particularly important to Jane, and vice versa. They were born in the same year, 1793, while Jane herself was still a teenager.

The first was Fanny Knight (Edward's family surname changed permanently to Knight after the death of his adoptive mother). Her mother Elizabeth died in 1808, when she was 15, leaving her the eldest of a tribe of children, and Jane was clearly a comfort, offering steady advice; later, she would also advise Fanny about love. She's the subject of one of Jane's rare effusions – in a late letter of February 1816, she wrote, 'You are the delight of my life. Such letters, such entertaining letters, as you have lately sent! Such a description of your queer little heart! Such a lovely display of what imagination does.'

The second was Anna, James Austen's only child with his first wife. Anna seems to have been something of a drama queen – charming, emotional and changeable, she felt neglected after her mother died, blaming her stepmother, Mary Lloyd, for favouring her own children. She was also an aspiring writer, an ambition ended by marriage – to Ben Lefroy, the son of Jane's friend, Madam Lefroy – and much childbearing. It was to Anna's younger sister, Caroline, that Jane wrote about the importance of aunts.

'A New Novel by a Lady'

TRYING AGAIN

With a settled base and enough time to write, Jane's attention turned again to the challenge of getting her work published. Her unsuccessful correspondence with Crosby had shown her that she couldn't, at least in the short term, get *Susan* back and publish it herself. It was time to look at the prospects of some of her other work.

By the autumn of 1810 the novel that had originally been *Elinor and Marianne* had been updated, revised and renamed *Sense and Sensibility*. Henry Austen, acting as his sister's agent, approached the London publisher Thomas Egerton with the book, and it was accepted for publication. Egerton, first and foremost a publisher of titles for a military readership – his imprint was The Military Library – was an unlikely choice for a contemporary novel; he was probably already a contact of Henry's, which would have made a deal easier to strike. Egerton's offer, too, was very much at the author's own risk: he was publishing on commission, which meant that Jane underwrote the cost of printing the book, and Egerton took a percentage on each book sold. Jane would only take a profit after both costs and percentage had been covered by sales. She may have been worried about writing a flop – she not only wanted but needed it to sell.

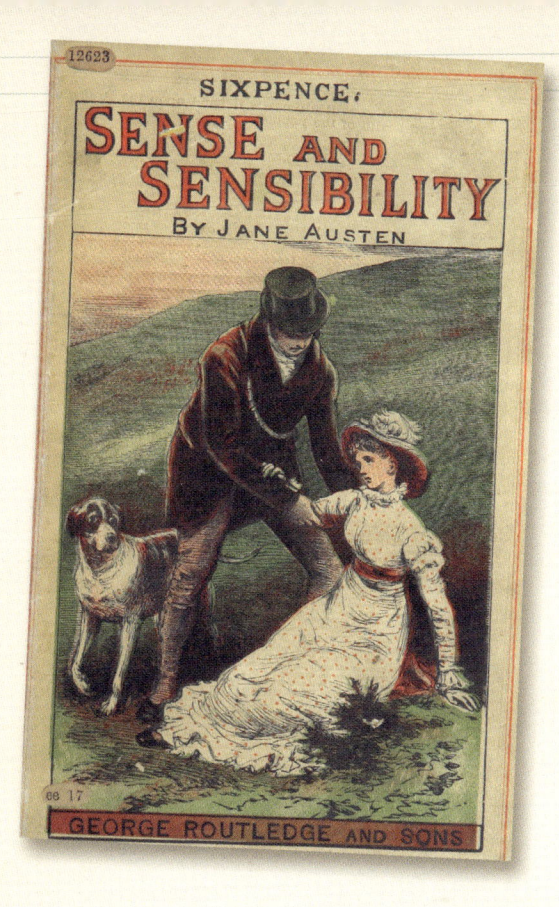

'No indeed, I am never too busy to think of S&S. I can no more forget it, than a mother can forget her sucking child.'

—Letter from Jane to Cassandra, who had evidently teased her that London pleasures were leading her to forget her proofs, 25 April 1811

Into Print

The printing process was long and frustrating. In March 1811 Jane stayed for a time at Henry and Eliza's house in London in order to correct her proofs, on the understanding that the book would be out in June, but the printing – at that date a laborious process done entirely by hand – dragged on. The book was finally advertised in October, an 'interesting work' in three volumes, costing 15 shillings. Jane remained anonymous – the book was 'By a Lady' and even, in a later, misprinted advertisement, 'By Lady A'. At long last, though, she was in print.

Print runs were very small by today's standards: the first edition of *Sense and Sensibility* was probably only around 750 copies. Nevertheless, it did well for a first novel; it received two positive reviews, and it had sold out by mid-1813. The interest it generated, like all books at the time, was mainly by word of mouth, but Jane's fears about having to reimburse the printer proved to be unfounded. When all the books had sold, she had made a profit of £140. The money – 'pewter' in her word – mattered; while it wasn't a huge amount, it was enough to give someone completely financially dependent a taste of freedom.

Above: By the end of the 19th century improved efficiencies in printing meant books became radically cheaper. This 1894 Routledge edition of *Sense and Sensibility* – its cover depicting a very Victorian Willoughby rescuing a bashful Marianne – cost a mere sixpence, a fraction of its debut price.

Opposite page: Engraving of a printing press – Napier's Platen Machine – from around 1820. Type was handset into frames, then pages were individually printed. Proofs had to be read and meticulously corrected by hand, and corrections made in the type before the final version could be printed.

A Published Author

'The incidents are probable, and highly pleasing and interesting.'

—From the review of *Sense and Sensibility* in *The Critical Review*, 1812

Interest in her book gradually grew. At home, her immediate family circle knew she had been published and she took her niece Caroline into her confidence, plus a few friends such as Anne Sharp and Edward Austen's benevolent adoptive mother, Mrs Knight, who had always taken an interest in Edward's 'other' family. Another niece, Anna Austen, who wasn't in on the secret, was reported to have picked *Sense and Sensibility* up while visiting the circulating library with her aunts, then put it down again, saying that she was sure it must be rubbish judging from the title. Jane and Cassandra were silently amused.

SEEKING PRAISE
Plenty of things would go on in much the same way after Austen was published, but one would not: she could no longer disguise her interest in what a wider audience felt about her book, and, having had some praise in a couple of reviews, became eager for more.

SENSE
AND
SENSIBILITY:

A NOVEL.

IN THREE VOLUMES.

BY A LADY.

VOL. I.

London:
PRINTED FOR THE AUTHOR,
By C. Roworth, Bell-yard, Temple-bar,
AND PUBLISHED BY T. EGERTON, WHITEHALL.
1811.

Success at Last
So far unknown to Jane, in London the book was becoming popular enough to be gossiped about. The apparent misprint in the second of Egerton's advertisements – 'By Lady A', rather than 'By a Lady' – led to discussions about which Lady A might have written it. *Sense and Sensibility* even reached junior royalty: Princess Charlotte, teenage daughter of the Regent, wrote to her friend that she identified with 'Maryanne', but was not so good (like any self-respecting teenager, she would have scorned to compare herself to prudent, cautious Elinor; she was also a fan of the wildly fashionable Byron).

The Next Step
Egerton may not have specialised in novels, but he was sharp enough to know when he had a hit on his hands; before the first print run sold out, he was considering Jane's next book. She had been reworking *First Impressions* for a while; she mentions that the length had been cut ('lopt and cropt'). It was time for it to be judged by the public. During the long wait for publication another novel had come out with the same name, so it also had a new title: *Pride and Prejudice*.

Top: *The Circulating Library* drawn by the cartoonist Isaac Cruikshank in the first decade of the 19th century.

Above: Popular Princess Charlotte, here shown as a teenager, was a keen novel reader.

'My Own Darling Child'

THE MOST POPULAR NOVEL 1812 was a busy year for Austen. She sold the completed *Pride and Prejudice* and was busy writing *Mansfield Park*. Thomas Egerton made a better offer for the successor to *Sense and Sensibility*: he was prepared to buy the copyright outright for £110.

The amount was less than Jane had hoped for, but as an arrangement it was uncomplicated and there was one immediate advantage – she didn't have to wait for the money, as she had to with the still-selling *Sense and Sensibility*.

'P.&P. is sold', she wrote to Martha Lloyd on 30 November, fitting the news in between family gossip and arrangements for Christmas: 'Egerton gives £110 for it. I would rather have had £150, but we could not both be pleased, & I am not at all surprised that he should not chuse to hazard so much. It's being sold will I hope be a great saving of Trouble to Henry… The Money is to be paid at the end of the twelvemonth.'

A Beginning and an End

There was a particular reason that Jane was keen to minimise the trouble to Henry. Eliza was ill, suffering serious symptoms from breast cancer. Charming as ever, she had visited Chawton Cottage with Henry for a couple of weeks in August, then continued to Godmersham, before travelling on to Ramsgate, with her French companion and a maid, to take the sea air.

In late January 1813 Jane received a finished copy of *Pride and Prejudice* at Chawton. Just as she had with *Sense and Sensibility*, she refers to it as her child; it must have been satisfying in a family so very full of mothers with growing families to have some finite productions of her own. Although she had maintained her anonymity, it would be this second book that would eventually reveal her as an authoress to a much wider public. For the moment, though, she could sit at home and look for the first positive reviews.

By April Eliza was critically ill. Henry collected Jane and brought her to London to be there for her cousin's last few days. It was a sad end to the glamorous figure who had made such an impression on Jane in childhood; she was only 50 when she died.

Below: Of all Austen's novels, *Pride and Prejudice* has had the greatest long-term popularity across the widest audience. It was quick to reprint, and her readers have consistently appreciated her more ridiculous characters – such as Mr Collins and Lady Catherine de Bourgh – while enjoying the slow-burn romance between the two leads.

'I want to tell you that I have got my own darling Child from London; on Wednesday I received one Copy... with three lines from Henry to say that he had given another to Charles & sent a 3d by the coach to Godmersham.'

—Letter from Jane to Cassandra, celebrating the arrival of the first copy of *Pride and Prejudice*, 29 January 1813

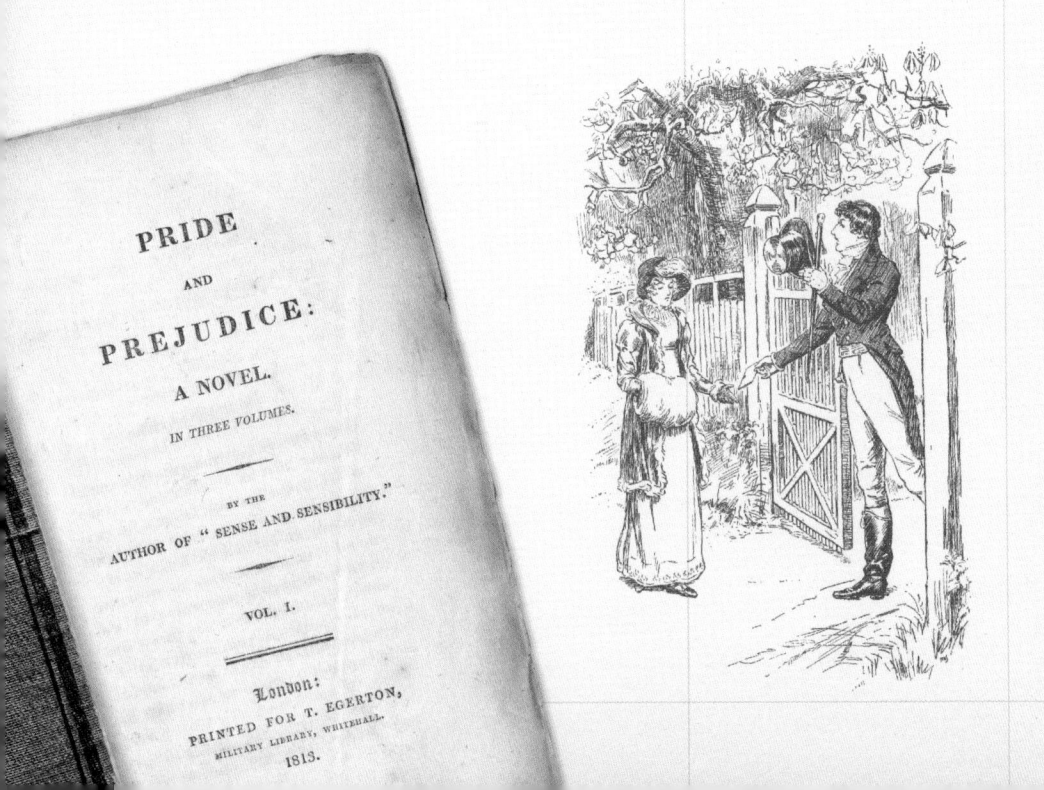

Chapter Five

Adventures in Publishing

How Publishing Worked

Higher Prices
When Egerton took on the risks of publishing Jane's second book, he also raised the price. *Pride and Prejudice* sold for 18 shillings, three shillings more than *Sense and Sensibility*. Selling the copyright had made for an easy deal, but in commercial terms it was a mistake for Austen – her flat-fee book would turn out to be a solid-gold crowd-pleaser.

Getting into Print

There were three ways for an author to get into print. Jane tried the first two – *Sense and Sensibility* was sold on commission and remained her property – the £140 she ultimately made belonged to her, and she was free to negotiate further editions with Egerton or another publisher as she chose. Egerton paid a specific sum for the copyright of *Pride and Prejudice*, after which the book belonged to him – if it did well, all the subsequent profits belonged to the publisher, although at that time copyright lasted for only 14 years after the book first came into print, after which it reverted to the author.

Finally, there was the subscription method – by which Jane had, long ago at Steventon, bought her copy of Fanny Burney's *Camilla* – when the author or their agent drew up an advertised subscription list and the customers who joined it paid for their book in advance, underwriting the expenses of production. This last option, while risk-free, was considered the least desirable – raising the money so directly was regarded as a slightly vulgar way for an author to go about things.

Left: A bookbinder working on a binding machine manufactured by Harrild & Sons in the early 1800s.

Below: 'The Circulating Library' in cartoon form, shown as a lady constructed entirely out of books.

Opposite page: Lackington and Allen, the most opulent circulating library in London, rumoured to stock over a million books, pictured in 1809.

Sometimes books might be published in more than one way; Burney raised £1,000 for *Camilla* on subscription but, shrewdly, subsequently sold the copyright to a publisher for a further £1,000, making it one of the most profitable books in a decade.

The Finished Product

Whichever arrangement had been made with the author, the book that a customer got for their money was in the form of two or three volumes in simple board bindings covered with paper. On a brand-new book, the pages were uncut – closed along the outer folds – and needed to be slit open with a paper knife.

Books had first been printed in multiple volumes at least partly to accommodate the circulating libraries – it meant that different readers could each borrow single volumes of titles at a time – so, in theory at least, three different people could be reading the book at once. Richer buyers would have plain new board-bound books re-bound more expensively to match the volumes in their libraries at home.

'The Advertisement is in our paper to day for the first time – 18's – He shall ask £1-1s for my two next, & £1-8's for my stupidest of all.'

—Letter from Jane to Cassandra, noting sarcastically that Egerton has put her price up, 29 January 1813

'A Very Superior Work'

Cost Cutting

With more of his own money on the line, Egerton ran more advertisements for *Pride and Prejudice* than he had for *Sense and Sensibility*, and mentioned that it was by the same author. He also used cheaper, thinner paper and crammed the type in tighter – ways to cut financial corners that, in future years, would cause tutting from John Murray who would become Austen's subsequent publisher.

Popular Success

Thin paper and cramped type didn't slow the novel down. The first edition sold out and a second went to press in the book's first year – without records, we have to guess the print runs, but they were probably around 750 copies each – and there were two very positive reviews, in *The British Critic* and *The Critical Review*, the same papers that had reviewed *Sense and Sensibility*.

Where *Pride and Prejudice* really took off was by word of mouth. Jane, down in Hampshire, commented on the reactions of those around her. Miss Benn, an impoverished neighbour and frequent visitor at Chawton was treated to a reading there one evening. 'She was amused, poor soul!' Jane tells Cassandra, going on '… she really does seem to admire Elizabeth. I must confess that I think her as delightful a creature as ever appeared in print…'

The Cleverest Thing

It must have been good to have the admiration of Miss Benn but elsewhere, bigger names were beginning to discuss Austen. The playwright Richard Brinsley Sheridan was said to have called the new novel one of the cleverest things he had ever read and – more importantly from an author's point of view – had told his friends to go and buy it.

On 1 May the heiress Annabella Milbanke, yet to set out on her disastrous marriage to Lord Byron, wrote to her mother, 'I have finished the novel called Pride and Prejudice, which I think a very superior work. It depends not on any of the common resources of Novel writers, no drownings, nor conflagrations… it is the most probable fiction I have ever read. It is not a crying book, but the interest is very strong, especially for Mr. Darcy.'

It may not have been a crying book, but Mr Darcy seems already to have been lined up with other romantic literary heroes.

Jane was up in London again – on the spot to be told what fashionable society was saying – later in 1813. She was staying with Henry, who, after Eliza's death, was arranging a move to smaller quarters, living over his office in Henrietta Street, Covent Garden.

Above left: Sheridan, one of the early enthusiasts for *Pride and Prejudice*....

Above right: ... and another, the intelligent and well-educated Annabella Milbanke.

Opposite page: A reluctant Elizabeth being presented to Mr Darcy as a dance partner in an illustration by Charles E. Brock for an 1895 edition of *Pride and Prejudice*.

The Moral Novel

BOOK THREE
Austen's third published novel was a marked departure from her first two. *Mansfield Park* **was begun in 1811 and finished by July 1813. It must have taken every spare minute she had; it was written over a period when there were many family calls on her time.**

This was the first book that she knew would go straight into print, but she also knew instinctively that it wasn't as much of a crowd-pleaser as *Pride and Prejudice*. The affairs of the Bertrams, a modern family in a great house, are seen through the eyes of their cousin, Fanny Price, adopted into the household as a child and occupying uneasy ground between servant and family. For today's reader the characters can be a problem – the morally compromised Mary and Henry Crawford, a brother and sister who arrive to be the disruptors at Mansfield, are so attractive that Fanny and Edmund Bertram, the 'hero' couple, can seem tiresomely priggish by contrast.

New Departures

There is plenty of compensatory brilliance: Austen uses the internal views of a whole range of characters, as well as her own, increasingly fearless, direct voice. In Mrs Norris, the malign aunt, she creates a memorable villain, and her satire, too, has hit full stride. Here, for example, is spoilt Maria Bertram – who has a strong fancy for amoral Henry Crawford – getting ready to marry the rich, stupid man to whom she is engaged. Austen sounds the marriage's death knell before it has even begun:

> *'I have something in hand – which I hope on the credit of P. & P. will sell well, tho' not half so entertaining.'*
>
> —Letter from Jane to Francis Austen on completing *Mansfield Park*, 6 July 1813

'In all the important preparations of the mind she was complete; being prepared for matrimony by an hatred of home… by the misery of disappointed affection and contempt of the man she was to marry. The rest might wait.'

It wasn't a favourite in the family circle – Mrs Austen found Fanny an insipid heroine, while Cassandra thought Jane should have married her to Henry Crawford. Perhaps she felt that a good wife might have been the saving of him.

Money Matters

Still, *Mansfield Park* sold well – published on 9 May 1814 and priced at 18 shillings, the print run of around 1,250 copies was sold out by November. We don't know whether Egerton made an offer for the copyright, but for this novel Jane went back to publishing on commission. It turned out to be a good decision because *Mansfield Park* was her best earner so far, making her a little over £300.

Above: Frontispiece to the 1906 edition, this one with plates by Harry Brock, a popular Edwardian illustrator of classic fiction.

Opposite page: Henry Crawford announcing to his sister Mary that he intends Fanny Price to fall in love with him, from an 1896 edition of *Mansfield Park* with illustrations by the artist Hugh Thomson.

Trips to London

COSMOPOLITAN LIFE
Jane Austen was a fairly frequent visitor to London. Her stays with Henry and Eliza, with their cosmopolitan friends and entertainments, had accustomed her to their sophisticated lifestyle, and after Eliza's death she continued to visit Henry regularly. Not only were there proofs to be checked, but there were also theatres, galleries and shops to be visited, and she enjoyed them to the full.

After her death, the enthusiasm of a younger generation of Austens for painting Jane as a sort of country mouse rather obscured this side to her, but her letters not only cover a lot of socialising and shopping – there are lists of commissions for everyone at Chawton – but also cultural outings, in particular theatre visits. At Steventon the Austens had had to do their own acting; in London she had the opportunity of seeing some of the great names of the age, including Edmund Kean and Mrs Jordan, on stage.

Cultural Pursuits

On a quiet morning at Henry's home in Henrietta Street in March 1814, Jane had 'read the Corsair, mended my petticoat, & [had] nothing else to do'. Byron's *Corsair*, only just out, was the season's publishing sensation, selling an unprecedented 10,000 copies on the day it appeared, although she sounds drily determined not to be too impressed. Fanny Knight was on this visit, too; a busier day saw them shopping and 'seeing the Indian Jugglers' – an acrobatic act performing at Pall Mall – in the morning, then dining at home before going to the theatre.

'We were quite satisfied with Kean...'

'My Gown is to be trimmed everywhere with white ribbon plaited on, somehow or other. She says it will look well. I am not sanguine. They trim with white very much.'

—Letter from Jane to Cassandra, dubious about her new London dress, 15 September 1813

In London, Jane was a frequent, informed theatregoer, and a critical one – on the same trip, she writes that Henry has secured hard-to-get tickets at Drury Lane to see 25-year-old Edmund Kean acting up a storm as Shylock in *The Merchant of Venice*. 'We were quite satisfied with Kean. I cannot imagine better acting, but the part was too short, & excepting him & Miss Smith… the parts were ill filled & the Play heavy.'

Miss Bennet in Paint

There were exhibitions, too. In May 1813, Jane tells Cassandra that she has looked for her characters in a collection of portraits – and has found Jane Bennet, 'Mrs Bingley is exactly herself, size, shaped face, features & sweetness; there never was a greater likeness.' (Researchers think that the portrait was probably of the fashionable Mrs Harriet Quentin who, not at all like Mrs Bingley, was a mistress of the Prince Regent).

Above: Fashionable dress for a ball in the 1810s.

Left: An engraving of the Huet-Villers portrait of Mrs Quentin, who Austen felt strongly resembled Jane Bennet.

Opposite page: Drury Lane Theatre, the largest in London, in 1808; this incarnation burned down just a year later, so Jane would have seen Edmund Kean, right, in the smaller rebuild that still stands today.

An End to Anonymity

ANONYMOUS WOMEN
Encouraged by her father and cheered on by her siblings, Austen never met with family opposition to her writing, although when she started out, anonymity was the genteel norm for women writers. The identities of those who persisted and were successful usually became known eventually, but during her lifetime none of her books was published under her name.

Indiscretions

Between 1812 and 1814, word that she was the author of *Sense and Sensibility*, *Pride and Prejudice* and, later, *Mansfield Park*, was gradually getting out. It had always been known in the family circle, but as the Austens were not particularly prominent socially her name didn't have any significance except in connection with her books. Although her brothers knew her preference for anonymity, the over-enthusiastic Henry never really stuck to it: whenever someone mentioned one of her novels, he couldn't resist telling them that his sister had written it.

Once her name was in circulation, it became part of the plentiful book gossip of the day. Over time, Jane became resigned to being known as an author, but it was difficult for someone who, unless she was completely comfortable with her company, mostly liked to observe. The role of celebrity didn't suit her, and when she talks about it, there's a rueful tone: on the one hand, she wants the credit for her work, on the other she dreads hearing something gauche or banal about it from an unsympathetic reader.

Writing for Income

In October 1814 Edward Knight was sued for possession of the Chawton estate by a neighbour who claimed the right to it through a knotty sequence of historical inheritance. Had the claim been successful, not only would he have had to hand over Chawton, but his sisters and mother would have lost their home, so the case was a nagging worry. Concerns about money made Jane even keener to earn as much as she could. The suit would only finally end in 1818, after Jane's death, when Edward paid the claimants off.

'... the truth is that the Secret has spread so far as to be scarcely the Shadow of a secret now – & that I believe whenever the 3rd [novel] appears, I shall not even attempt to tell lies about it. – I shall rather try to make all the Money than all the Mystery I can out of it.'

—Letter from Jane to Francis Austen, beginning to appreciate the value of her name, 25 September 1813

Left: *Writing*, painted ca. 1905-9, by the US artist Gari Melchers.

Emma

FREE CHOICES
Austen began work on the character she thought 'no-one but myself will very much like' in January 1814. Unlike any previous Austen heroine, Emma Woodhouse – young, rich, handsome and smug – is free to make her own choices, and the great joy of the novel is watching her make a hash of them.

Like *Mansfield Park*, *Emma* was a modern novel, much concerned with its different characters' autonomy. Although it's a comedy of errors, the figure at their centre is invariably Emma herself – long before she reaches any degree of self-awareness, the reader sees what should, and must, happen. The intricacies of the plot seem effortless: Austen at the peak of her skill.

Realistic Heroines

Did Jane Austen, now not far off 40, draw on any of the younger generation to create charming, self-satisfied Emma? The two nieces that she was closest to, Anna Austen and Fanny Knight, might each have loaned a little to her heroine's personality. Anna was wilful, dynamic and attractive; she had made a huge fuss about being denied permission to be courted by one young man, only to reject him when her father

Right: A widowed Anna Lefroy, painted in 1845 by the miniaturist Richard Ubsdell.

Opposite page: Engraving of Hans Place in 1800, a few years before Henry Austen moved there, showing the still-rural neighbourhood.

and her disliked stepmother relented. By early 1815 she was newly married to Ben Lefroy – another suitor of whom the family had not wholly approved.

Fanny, on the other hand, was the original girl with everything: an indulgent father who didn't let financial worries impact on his family, plenty of pin money and, like Emma, 'very little to distress or vex her', although, again like Emma, she was motherless. Austen may have borrowed something from both girls, and their frequent letters and visits must have been helpful with youthful expressions and conversation – but in the end, Emma Woodhouse is a solid enough personality to seem entirely convincing in her own right.

Time to Write

In the summer of 1814 Henry Austen moved out of the rooms above his office and took a house in Hans Place, in what is now Knightsbridge. Jane enjoyed spending time there that summer and autumn – she could work in Henry's library, with a door leading directly into the garden when she wanted a break. It must have been refreshing to have a little time to herself without the domestic interruptions inevitable at Chawton. She completed *Emma* in the spring of 1815, after little more than a year's work.

'I live in his room downstairs, it is particularly pleasant, from opening upon the garden. I go & refresh myself every now and then, and then come back to Solitary Coolness.'

—Letter from Jane to Cassandra, on the pleasures of time to herself, 23 August 1814

A Civil Rogue

A New Publisher

Thomas Egerton was Jane Austen's publisher for her first three books by default – he had taken her on at a time when there were no other options. For *Emma*, she made a change. Egerton made an offer, she didn't consider it good enough, and Henry approached John Murray, the celebrity publisher of the day.

The business had been founded by Murray's father, and the son was taking it from strength to strength: he published Walter Scott and Lord Byron, and *The Quarterly Review*, which covered political and philosophical discussion as well as reviewing new books. Despite this, he didn't have a lot of experience with novels. When Henry Austen approached him, he asked William Gifford, editor of the *Review*, to read the proposed book. Gifford was enthusiastic – and clearly recognised the inimitable Austen style – 'Of *Emma*, I have nothing but good to say', he wrote, 'I was sure of the author before you mentioned her.'

Negotiations

John Murray duly made an offer. The figure was £450 – but it was for three books, not one. He wanted the copyrights for *Sense and Sensibility* and *Mansfield Park* included in the deal. Henry was quick to refuse, expressing incredulity at the offer's meanness – 'The Terms you offer are so very inferior to what we had expected that I am apprehensive of having made some great Error…'

'Mr Murray's Letter is come; he is a Rogue of course, but a civil one. He offers £450 but wants to have the Copyright of MP. & S&S included. It will end in my publishing for myself I dare say. He sends more praise however than I expected. It is an amusing Letter.'

—Letter from Jane to Cassandra, 17 October 1815

Mid-negotiation, Henry fell seriously ill. He was sick enough for Jane, staying with him, to summon James, Edward and Cassandra to Hans Place. Henry rallied but was convalescent for a time, and Jane stayed on, both to supervise his recovery and to sort out the agreement for *Emma*. In the end she agreed to a commission deal, with the standard 10 per cent going to Murray, along with a second edition of *Mansfield Park* on the same terms. She was ready to take on the business of being an author for herself.

Below: John Murray (far left), with (far right) the editor and satirist William Gifford who also acted as Murray's informal 'reader'. The pair sandwich two of Murray's most celebrated (male) clients – on the left, Walter Scott, in silhouette and, next to him, Lord Byron, in a romantic portrait of 1813 by Richard Westall.

The Regent's Librarian

SICKROOM GOSSIP
Dr Baillie, who looked after Henry during his illness, was also doctor to the Prince Regent. No sooner had Jane's brother recovered enough to chat then, as usual, he shared the 'secret' that his sister had authored some of the decade's most popular novels. Dr Baillie, in return, enthused about them and shared back that the Regent, a keen novel reader, was an admirer of Austen's work.

Jane wasn't flattered by the news; she had no love for 'Prinny', by now into his corpulent fifties and wildly unpopular with the public. After some polite toing and froing, though, the Prince's librarian, Dr James Stanier Clarke, called, and invited her to make a prestigious visit to the library at the Regent's London home, Carlton House. She went, and Clarke, a wonderfully absurd figure, became a fan himself.

Ideas and Suggestions

For once, we have both sides of the correspondence – Clarke's letters and Jane's replies. He offers her the use of his own library, along with absurd suggestions for characters and plots, many based on himself, that she might use. His style, full of high-flown compliments and French phrases, makes them a joy to read, while her letters back are full of modest and probably insincere disclaimers: '… I think I may boast myself to be, with all possible Vanity, the most unlearned, & uninformed Female who ever dared to be an Authoress'. You can hear her laughing behind her hand.

Left: Dr Baillie attended Henry Austen and the Prince Regent.

Below: Here painted by Sir Thomas Lawrence, and looking rather florid, by 1815 the Prince Regent was showing signs of his dissipated lifestyle and had become increasingly unpopular with the public.

Opposite top: James Stanier Clarke, the Prince's librarian, painted in around 1790 by John Russell.

Opposite bottom: This watercolour from Stanier Clarke's commonplace book – in which he both wrote and painted – is believed by some scholars to be a portrait of Jane Austen. The features bear a resemblance to Cassandra's portrait; the face has been cut out and collaged onto a figure in an extravagantly fashionable costume.

The Dedication

One unwelcome result of the meeting was the suggestion – really a command – that Jane dedicate her new book, *Emma*, to the Prince. Not only did this mean a more fulsome dedication than she liked – quietly dropped from later editions – but she also had to pay out of her own pocket for a finely bound presentation copy for the royal library.

There's a footnote to the story. Clarke may not have played the role he wanted in Jane's writing, but he did inspire a sharp little piece from her for the private entertainment of family and friends. Called *The Plan of a Novel, According to Hints from Various Quarters*, it incorporated some of his silliest suggestions, along with a few, equally ridiculous, from other sources.

'Pray continue to write, & make all your friends send Sketches to help you – and Memoires pour servir as the French term it. Do let us have an English Clergyman after your fancy... and describe him burying his own mother – as I did – because the High Priest of the Parish... did not pay her remains the respect he ought to do.'

—Letter from James Stanier Clarke to Jane, getting carried away by his own ideas, 21 December 1815

The Crash

BANKRUPTCY

1816 opened badly for the Austen family – in March, Henry's bank crashed, victim of the economic instability that marked the end of the Napoleonic Wars and possibly also overstretched by Henry's own optimism. Henry was declared bankrupt, and the ripples affected the whole family.

Family Losses

Mr Leigh-Perrot – Mrs Austen's Bath brother – and Edward Knight had both acted as guarantors for Henry when he was appointed receiver-general for Oxfordshire taxes (a sort of local link between parish tax collection and the Exchequer) just the year before, the former for the considerable amount of £10,000 and the latter for an enormous £20,000. Both lost their money. Two of the other Austen brothers, James and Frank, also made losses and even Jane was affected, losing around £26, part of her earnings from *Mansfield Park*.

The tight-knit Austens closed ranks, but the brothers' losses made it harder for them to subsidise the household at Chawton Cottage and must have added to feelings of instability that had already been raised by the suit against Edward. There would probably also have been a degree of social shame in Henry's failure. The only outside mention we hear is Jane's request to John Murray, in a letter of 1 April, that he send any correspondence directly to her at Chawton 'in consequence of the late sad Event in Henrietta St…' After that, there's a gap in her letters, other than brief notes to her nephews and nieces, until September; family commentary was probably among the correspondence burned by Cassandra.

Resurrection

Henry had phoenix-like qualities: completely ruined, he left his office and the Hans Place house and pragmatically rediscovered an attraction to the church. Before long he was ordained by the Bishop of Winchester, and nine months after the crash he was settling in as a curate at Chawton, with a small but viable income, just in time to preach the Christmas sermon. In Jane's letters he is referred to with her customary affection: he visits and dines with them often, and her bond with her favourite brother seems close as ever – after all, she, too, had benefited from his success. A late portrait made of him in clerical dress shows a handsome man very like the description of his late father, with the same fine eyes, straight nose and white, thistledown hair.

Below: The church at Chawton, with Chawton House shown in the background, painted in 1809. Henry became curate here at the end of 1816.

Opposite page: Economic uncertainties at the end of the Napoleonic Wars caused ructions that affected most financial institutions from the Bank of England downwards. Henry Austen's was just one of the small country banks that suffered.

'Uncle Henry writes very superior Sermons. You & I must try to get hold of one or two, & put them into our Novels; it would be a fine help to a volume; & we could make our Heroine read it aloud of a Sunday Evening...'

—Letter from Jane to her nephew James Edward, who also had writing ambitions, 16 December 1816

Local Opinion

UNDER THE SPOTLIGHT
The better Jane became known as an author at home, the more opinions on her work she would hear from friends and neighbours, and the closer the scrutiny to which she would be subjected – far greater than when she had been simply one half of the spinster Austen sisters.

More people might want to meet Jane, but she didn't necessarily want to meet them. As early as May 1813 she was writing to Cassandra, upon hearing that the rich, social Miss Burdett wished to meet her, 'I should like to see Miss Burdett very well, but that I am rather frightened by hearing that she wishes to be introduced to *me*. If I am a wild Beast, I cannot help it. It is not my own fault.'

A Silent Observer

Now, even people in her Chawton neighbourhood might decide that they wanted a closer look. According to an amusing but surely malicious account by Mary Russell Mitford, a now-largely-forgotten local writer and essayist, those people might not get much reward for their efforts. In 1815 Mitford quoted a friend who visited Chawton Cottage and reported that Jane observed the company in silence:

'A friend of mine, who visits her now, says that... till "Pride and Prejudice" showed what a precious gem was hidden in that unbending case, she was no more regarded in society than a poker or a fire-screen... The case is very different now; she is still a poker – but a poker of whom every one is afraid.'

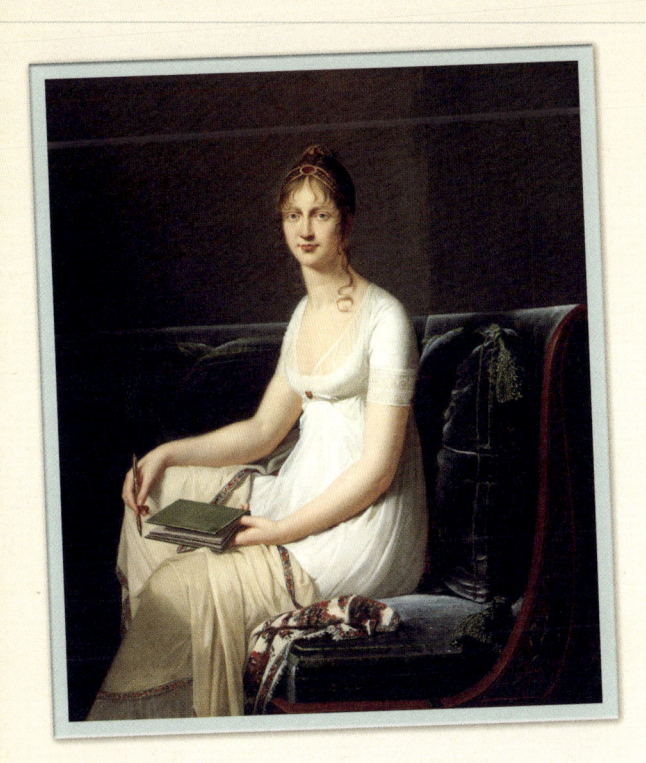

Left: The accomplishments of young ladies, exclaimed over by Mr Bingley in *Pride and Prejudice*, and, predictably, denigrated by Mr Darcy, included sketching – like this fashionable sitter painted by Lefévre in 1808 – singing, playing instruments and a good deal of reading of both the improving and the less improving kind. It's hardly surprising that book gossip was a common topic of conversation.

Opposite page: Mary Russell Mitford, well known in her day as an essayist, novelist, dramatist – and gossip – but whose works have now sunk into obscurity.

It seems that Miss Austen was still not performing to strangers. In mitigation, the 'friend' quoted was a member of the family who were suing Edward Knight for the Chawton estate, so was unlikely to have been treated to much of Jane's sparkling conversation.

The Opinion Books

She remained, though, very engaged by all opinions, good or bad, of her novels. For *Mansfield Park* and *Emma*, she made collections of the comments she heard. The two booklets – cut down from larger sheets and folded into the small notebooks she always used – are now in the British Library. Far from concentrating on the positive, Jane has written down every view she has ever heard, from those of prominent people to neighbours, and from the thoughtful and sensitive to the outright ridiculous. Some of them are the sort of passing comment that one wishes no author ever had to hear. Mrs August Bramstone, slogging through *Mansfield Park*, managed to insult Austen's entire output:

'Mrs August Bramstone – Owned that she thought S. & S. – and P. & P. downright nonsense, but expected to like M.P. better, & having finished the 1st vol. – flattered herself she had got through the worst.'

Sales, Reviews and Money

A Poor Return

Austen may have traded up when she joined the publisher John Murray, but this wasn't reflected in the work she had to do, or in financial terms. With *Emma* in preparation, she is still complaining about how slow the printer is with her proofs, and the undoubted clout that Murray had in contemporary literary circles didn't result in profit.

Star Reviewer

An optimistic print run for *Emma* – 2,000 copies – was generated by good sales for *Mansfield Park*. *Emma* came in three volumes and cost a guinea, publishing on 23 December 1815. The 750-copy second edition of *Mansfield Park* appeared in February 1816. Both used heavier paper and were better printed than the Egerton publications; Murray didn't believe in cutting corners.

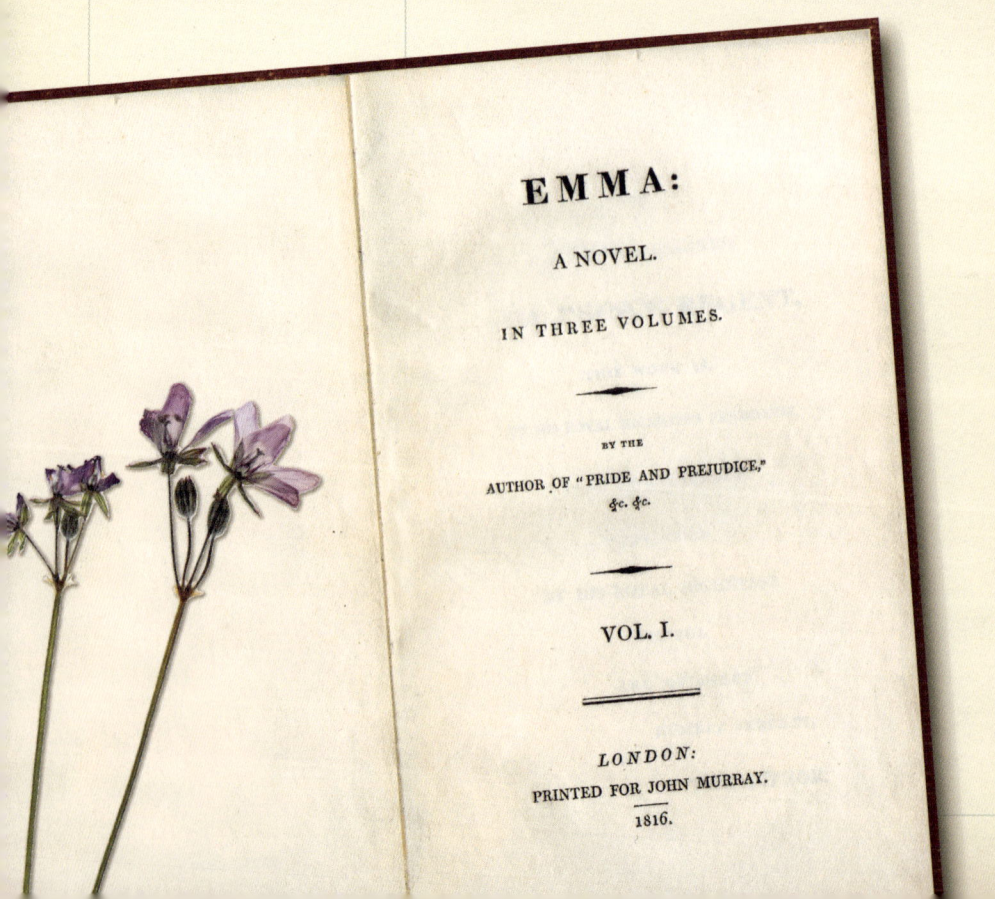

It was at Murray's suggestion, too, that Walter Scott wrote an extended review of *Emma* in the (Murray-owned) *Quarterly Review*. Already a highly regarded poet, Scott had recently also become a celebrated novelist, having published *Waverley*, much admired by Jane, in 1814. His piece was the first thoughtful discussion of Austen's strengths by a fellow writer, and it covers *Sense and Sensibility* and *Pride and Prejudice* as well – although not *Mansfield Park*, the book which particularly needed a sales boost and which, alone of Jane's novels, was not reviewed on its first appearance. Jane expressed her dismay directly to Murray: 'The Authoress of *Emma* has no reason I think to complain of her treatment in it – except in the total omission of *Mansfield Park*.' Scott is impressed by Austen's originality in her naturalistic treatment of characters and situations – he identifies a genuine pioneer.

> 'The author's knowledge of the world, and the peculiar tact with which she presents characters that the reader cannot fail to recognize, reminds us something of the merits of the Flemish school of painting.'

—Walter Scott, *The Quarterly Review*, dated October 1815 (published March 1816)

Disappointment

Emma sold well, but not well enough to reflect the larger print run – 1,248 copies had sold by October 1816, and over 500 copies would eventually be remaindered in 1820, long after Jane's death. Even these sales would have netted Jane over £300, but the second edition of *Mansfield Park* sold very poorly indeed. When Murray eventually wrote her a cheque on 21 October 1816 it was for a niggardly £38 18s; the losses on the printing of *Mansfield Park* had been a drag on the profits of *Emma*.

Creatively, Austen had allowed herself no let-up. She had completed *Persuasion* in the interim, and thoroughly revised *Susan*, the rights finally bought back from Crosby. Jane was now referring to it as 'Miss Catherine', although it would ultimately be published as *Northanger Abbey*.

Above left: Prodded by John Murray, Walter Scott, here painted by Raeburn in 1822, wrote a warm review of Austen's work, but for some reason left *Mansfield Park* out of his overview, vexing Austen who felt it was the one of her books that specifically needed the publicity.

Opposite page: Title page of the first edition of *Emma*, which was ultimately remaindered after a quarter of the initial print run failed to sell.

The Last Novel

MATURE WORK
The work that Austen was doing in the cool library at Hans Place in the autumn months of 1815 was probably at least in part on *Persuasion*. It was the last novel she would complete; started in early August, it was finished almost exactly a year later, by when the days of trips to London were over.

Austen's Improvements

This is the only novel in which Jane's own editing survives. For the last two chapters of *Persuasion*, the denouement in which Anne Elliot, Austen's older-and-wiser heroine, finds that Captain Wentworth is still in love with her, in fact has never fallen out of love with her, we have both the original and the author's rewrite.

In the first version Wentworth makes a direct declaration, but Jane seems to have decided that the scenes lacked tension, and the final version has a more intricate setup, in which Anne, in discussing love with another character, Captain Harville, is sending coded messages to Wentworth, who is in the same room. He listens to her, realises that she still feels for him, and writes one of Austen's great fictional letters, a feverish declaration of love which brings the novel to a triumphantly romantic conclusion.

'I offer myself to you again with a heart even more your own than when you almost broke it, eight years and a half ago. Dare not say that man forgets sooner than woman, that his love has an earlier death. I have loved none but you.'

—From Captain Wentworth's love letter to Anne Elliot, *Persuasion*, 1817

Naval Lives

Persuasion has also been called Austen's love letter to the British Navy. She began it just after Napoleon's final defeat, bringing the wars with the French, which had been going on almost all her adult life, to an end. She was following her own advice, to write about what she knew: Frank and Charles Austen had successful naval careers, and she had lived for two years in Southampton, where she would have been steeped in naval conversation and observation. Almost all her sailors, from William Price to Captain Wentworth, are estimable, and the novel is full of admiration for the ingenuity and level-headedness of navy men, their working lives full of difficulties and danger far from home. Ebullient Louisa Musgrove may have been expressing Jane Austen's feelings as well as Anne Elliot's when, naturally more gushing than either, she '[bursts] forth into raptures of admiration and delight on the character of the navy; their friendliness, their brotherliness, their openness, their uprightness…' after a happy afternoon with Wentworth and his fellow officers.

Above: Captain Wentworth helping Anne out with her childcare duties: an engraving from the 1821 French edition of *Persuasion*, *La Famille Elliot*.

Opposite page: A Brock illustration from 1898, showing Captain Wentworth passing his letter, with its declaration of love, to Anne.

CHAPTER SIX

ILLNESS, DEATH AND LEGACY

Fading Health

The First Signs
At some point early in 1816 there begin to be regular mentions of Jane feeling unwell. Just a few hints in the beginning, scattered through her own letters and those of close family members: Aunt Jane has trouble with her eyes; she has a fever; her back hurts; though 'perfectly well' she does not feel up to walking a mile home from a supper party, and so on.

Too Busy to be Ill
These sort of vague symptoms would have been commonplace heard from Mrs Austen – who had suffered from a confusing mixture of hypochondria and occasional serious illness for decades – but Jane had rarely spoken of her health. Although she never seems to be quite well, she isn't spared from nursing Henry, sorting out her publishing affairs, offering thoughtful advice to Fanny Knight and to James Austen's son, James Edward, both of whom were aspiring writers, and, of course, getting on with her own work. In June 1816, however, Cassandra was worried enough to take her sister to Cheltenham, then a popular spa town, to take the waters. Jane said that it had helped – but she still wasn't well.

Ready for Publication

She wasn't pushing her new work forward, either. Having rewritten those last two chapters of *Persuasion* (referred to as *The Elliots*; we don't know whether she or someone else came up with the novel's final title), and recast *Catherine*, including a short note to future readers explaining why the novel might seem a little dated, Austen doesn't seem to have taken further action to get them into print. Perhaps she was too tired to start on a round of negotiations, maybe Henry's reinvention as a curate meant that he had no time to help her in managing John Murray – there's nothing to tell us. In two late letters to Fanny Knight, both from March 1817, she mentions that she has finished her latest project, and has shared the news with James Austen, but there's no evidence that she got as far as sending the new work to her publisher.

In the second of these letters, she also mentions that she needs to take long rests when out walking, but 'I mean to take to riding the Donkey' so that she can accompany Cassandra on walks (sparking a jollier memory for the reader of Mrs Elton's strawberry-picking excursion to Donwell Abbey in *Emma*).

'Miss Catherine is put upon the Shelve for the present... but I have a something ready for Publication, which may perhaps appear about a twelvemonth hence... This is for yourself alone.'

—Letter from Jane to Fanny Knight, announcing *Persuasion*, 13 March 1817

Left: 1825 drawing by the cartoonist Robert Cruikshank, showing the busy Cheltenham street outside the entrance to the wells where Jane would have gone to drink the waters.

Something New: Sanditon

The Last Manuscript

She continued working into early 1817. In January she began *The Brothers*, later published as *Sanditon*. Over the next few weeks she wrote 12 chapters, a total of around 23,000 words, before laying down her pen on 18 March, writing the date neatly at the end of the manuscript. She must, finally, have felt too tired to go on.

Fresh Departures

There are hints in the fragment that *Sanditon* would have been as innovative as all her other novels. Instead of her much-quoted '3 or 4 families in a country village' as subject matter, with this book she seems to have intended to capture a whole town – a rapidly developing community, caught just at the point of its transformation from a fishing village to a new seaside resort. Buildings are going up *en masse*, and shops stocked for a newly broad range of customers, while the cast of characters includes, among many others, a feckless lord; a local landowner-turned-property speculator; Lady Denham, queen bee of her small social circle; and Miss Lambe, a West Indian heiress, just 17, 'chilly and tender' (and Austen's only non-white character). In Charlotte Heywood, the outside observer, landed in Sanditon through chance, she has also created a likeable and unaffected heroine.

'Charlotte... found amusement enough in standing at her ample Venetian window and looking over the miscellaneous foreground of unfinished buildings, waving linen and tops of houses, to the sea, dancing and sparkling in sunshine and freshness.'

—Charlotte Heywood, enjoying her first day in the new resort, *Sanditon*, written 1817, first published 1925

Even the very rough draft that remains contains plenty of short, scene-setting landscape descriptions – rare in Austen until the first glimpses of Lyme in *Persuasion*, and seemingly to be further developed in the new book. Her love of the seaside finds its way appealingly onto the page.

Old and New

However innovative Jane's novels were, she always followed the advice that she had given to Anna Austen when her niece was trying out her own story, to stick to what she knew. When Anna considered sending her characters out of the country, Jane was cautious. 'Let the Portmans go to Ireland, but as you know nothing of the Manners there, you had better not go with them', she recommended.

When it came to bathing resorts, however, she had all those summer holidays with her parents to draw on and was on terms of comfortable familiarity with the everyday habits of both locals and visitors. All the ingredients for another masterpiece had been put in place; as it turned out, the only thing missing was the time to put them together.

Right: A fashion illustration from 1814, showing a 'Circassian ladies corset and sea side bathing dress' (sic) – one hopes the much-trimmed top layer was removed before the lady took to the water.

Opposite page: The Dorset coastline between Lyme and Charmouth, shown in the early 19th century – *Sanditon*, while set instead in an imagined part of Sussex, is about developing a resort in unspoiled surroundings such as these.

Rapid Decline

Last Glimpse of Aunt Jane
By the end of March 1817 Jane was losing strength. There's a sad little account from James Austen's daughter Caroline, aged 12 when her aunt died, of the last visit she paid her, finding the invalid sitting up in the bedroom where she was spending most of her time.

The Will

The four surviving letters Jane wrote in March range widely and humorously over all sorts of matters as well as her health, her fine, even handwriting unchanged. On 21 April, though, she made her will. She wrote just 12 lines; there are two legacies of £50 each, one for Henry and one for Madame Bigeon, a faithful servant of Henry and Eliza's household who had originally accompanied Eliza over from France and who Jane had come to know well over the years. Everything else went to Cassandra, who was also appointed her executrix.

On 22 May she wrote a last letter from Chawton, to Anne Sharp, Fanny Knight's old governess, who had become her close friend. She is still counting her blessings vigorously – 'I can sit up in my bed & employ myself… I have so many alleviations & comforts to bless the Almighty for!' – but also gives a much fuller account of her illness, mentioning the visit of Mr Lyford, a Winchester physician, who believes he can cure her if she moves nearer the hospital and his services.

'... She... kindly greeted us – and then pointing to seats which had been arranged for us by the fire, she said, "There's a chair for the married lady, and there's a little stool for you, Caroline." It is strange but those trifling words are the last of hers that I can remember.'

—Caroline Austen, recalling the shock of finding how ill her aunt was, *My Aunt, Jane Austen: A Memoir*, written in 1867

What Killed Jane?

The symptoms mentioned over the last year or so of Austen's life are so various that contemporary experts have held a long debate over what killed her: the range of possibilities have included Addison's disease, Bright's disease and various cancers including Hodgkin lymphoma. She had a longstanding problem with her eyes – probably conjunctivitis – and pains in her face. She also complains of skin discolouration: '… black and white and every wrong colour. I must not depend upon being ever very blooming again,' she writes to Fanny Knight on 23 March.

Looking back more than two centuries, it's unlikely we'll ever know for sure. What is comfortably certain is that her family did everything possible to help; she had the devoted care of Cassandra, and the interest and affection of her brothers, nephews and nieces – and even of her often-caustic mother.

Right: An early 19th-century visit to the apothecary. 'Doses' could be purchased for most everyday ailments (and a visit from the apothecary would usually be cheaper than a visit from the doctor). In Winchester Jane consulted the greater expertise of Giles Lyford, a well-regarded physician and the nephew of John Lyford who had been the Austen family's doctor at Steventon.

Opposite page: Jane Austen's will. The fact that it was unwitnessed meant that it was technically illegal, which caused delays after her death.

Death in Winchester

Last Journey
On 27 May 1817 Jane left for Winchester, riding in James's carriage, attended by Cassandra, and with Henry and William, Edward Austen's son, on horseback, riding alongside. Her old friend Elizabeth Bigg, now Mrs Heathcote, widowed and living in Winchester, had found the sisters lodgings in College Street.

The Final Few Days
Once there, they settled into the modest rooms. One or two letters tell us that she has been taken out in a sedan chair, and that Mr Lyford is helping her to get better. She rallied for a little while, and there were visits from Charles Austen and from Mary, James's wife, who came twice to relieve Cassandra by watching over Jane at night. The family were careful that old Mrs Austen received only positive news, but by this time no one thought that Jane could recover. On 15 July she dictated a poem to Cassandra, to mark St Swithin's Day, but two days later had some kind of seizure or crisis. Mr Lyford came to administer laudanum, the favoured painkiller of the day, and she died in the small hours of 18 July.

Right: The cramped College Street lodgings where Jane Austen died on 18 July 1817.

Opposite page: An 1894 Hugh Thomson illustration for *Pride and Prejudice*, showing Elizabeth reading her sister's letters. Cassandra stayed in constant communication with the extended family by letter during Jane's final days.

> *'I have lost a treasure, such a Sister, such a friend as never can have been surpassed, She was the sun of my life, the gilder of every pleasure, the soother of every sorrow, I had not a thought concealed from her, & it is as if I had lost a part of myself.'*
>
> —Letter from Cassandra to Fanny Knight, 20 July 1817

Last Rites

Cassandra, usually the more prosaic of the sisters, paid a feeling tribute to Jane in a letter to Fanny Knight – much-quoted, it is eloquent with both her love and her grief. The body lay in an open coffin in College Street while an interment in Winchester Cathedral was quickly arranged – Mrs Heathcote's late husband had served there, and of course Henry's recent ordination had been made by the Bishop, so there may have been strings to pull.

Early in the morning of 24 July – to avoid disrupting the 10 o'clock service – Henry, Francis, Charles and James's son James Edward accompanied the coffin to the Cathedral, and Jane was interred there in a vault under the nave. Women didn't generally attend funerals, and Cassandra stayed at home.

We don't know who composed the inscription for the stone set over her vault, but although it pays due tribute to her piety, benevolence, sweet temper and intelligence, it doesn't mention her writing.

The 'Biographical Note'

SPECIAL EDITION
No time was wasted in getting Austen's unpublished works into print. *Catherine* – now *Northanger Abbey* – and *Persuasion* were produced together in a four-volume 'special' by John Murray, publishing on 20 December 1817. Jane's first and last novels now literally bookended her work.

Cassandra was clearly an efficient literary executor; her main concern may have been in getting Jane's remaining work out to the public, but the Chawton household – as usual – was short of money. Murray paid £500 for both titles and mentions them in a letter to Byron, written on 9 September. He is listing publications for the forthcoming season (he was trying to coax the fourth canto of *Childe Harold's Pilgrimage*, Byron's madly successful narrative work, out of the late-delivering poet) and says the list includes 'Two new Novels left by Miss Austen – the ingenious Author of *Pride & Prejudice* – who I am sorry to say died about 6 weeks ago.'

A Dutiful Woman

Henry Austen added a biographical note to the new books, finally putting the official stamp of author on Jane – the sister whose cover he had unofficially blown so often in her lifetime. His contribution, with its stress on Jane's modesty, her attention to duty, and her domestic virtues, grates a bit today – possibly unwittingly he has set up a sweet, kindly and bland characterisation that would endure well into the 20th century and which sometimes still crops up today.

NORTHANGER ABBEY:
AND
PERSUASION.

BY THE AUTHOR OF "PRIDE AND PREJUDICE,"
"MANSFIELD-PARK," &c.

WITH A BIOGRAPHICAL NOTICE OF THE AUTHOR.

IN FOUR VOLUMES.
VOL. I.

LONDON:
JOHN MURRAY, ALBEMARLE-STREET.
1818.

'Short and easy will be the task of the mere biographer. A life of usefulness, literature, and religion, was not by any means a life of event.'

—From the Biographical Notice by Henry Austen – painting Jane as a bit too good to be true

Left: One of the Hugh Thomson illustrations – this one, from 1897, for *Northanger Abbey* – which enhanced Austen's popularity into the Edwardian era.

Opposite page: The title page of Murray's edition combining *Northanger Abbey* and *Persuasion*, which came out just five months after Jane's death.

'We have always regarded [Austen's] works as possessing a higher claim to public estimation than perhaps they have yet attained. They have fallen, indeed, upon an age whose taste can only be gratified with the highest seasoned food.'

—An astute reviewer spots that Jane's skill is underestimated because of the fashion for the sensational, *Blackwood's Edinburgh Magazine*, May 1818

Fresh Reviews

Now that the literary world officially knew who Austen was, it could mourn her loss – and the two new novels sparked more reviews of her work overall than any of her previous works. Several were thoughtful looks at Austen's skills and at the sheer novelty of her style: the realism of her cast, the naturalness of her situations, and the fact that her female characters in particular were so varied, yet also so far from the pictures of perfection that had been commonplace in novels before hers. Many were far more perspicacious than Henry's fulsome but reductive tribute.

Cassandra and Jane

KEEPER OF THE LEGACY
Cassandra Austen went on living at Chawton for the rest of her life; she survived her sister by 28 years. She was conscientious in looking after the legacy she'd been left, and although modern scholars lament her destruction of so many of Jane's letters, this was likely what Jane herself would have wanted.

The Uncompleted Deal

Jane's works were safely into print, but Thomas Egerton was now dead, and *Pride and Prejudice* was stuck with his estate, separated from the rest of her books. Gradually her works sold out and were not reprinted – by 1830 they were all out of print. In May 1831 Cassandra wrote to John Murray, responding to a letter that must have proposed buying the copyright for all the books and bringing out a complete set. It's careful and detailed; she says that she does not want to give the rights up and asks a lot of questions: will he undertake to buy the rights for *Pride and Prejudice* from Egerton, what will he offer for a commission deal, how big would the edition be, how much will it cost, when will it come out, and so on. At the time Murray was trying to put together affordable sets of books for a wider readership and was under some pressure financially; clearly the negotiations failed, leaving the way open for Richard Bentley a year later.

> As I have leisure, I am looking over and destroying some of my papers – others I have marked "to be burned", whilst some will still remain. These are chiefly a few letters and a few manuscripts of our dear Jane, which I have set apart for those parties to whom I think they will be most valuable.

—Letter from Cassandra to Charles Austen, 9 May 1843

Illness, Death and Legacy 145

Left: One of only two verified images of Jane Austen – a back view, painted in watercolour by Cassandra in 1804.

Opposite page: Elizabeth's confrontation with Lady Catherine de Bourgh, engraved as the frontispiece for the 1833 edition of *Pride and Prejudice*, which was published by Richard Bentley after Henry and Cassandra's negotiations with John Murray failed.

Sorting Things Out

After her mother's death and Martha's marriage, Cassandra became known as a benevolent, devout old lady in Chawton village – living alone, visiting relatives and remembered for holding sewing and reading classes for local girls – and also for owning a 'nice dog, Link' who would accompany her servant to collect the milk from a nearby farm daily, and carry the pail back in his mouth. Not hygienic, perhaps, but charming all the same.

In 1843 she wrote her will, appointing Charles, the youngest sibling, as her executor. At the same time she went through Jane's papers, leaving the three books of Juvenilia and some separate bits and pieces to individual siblings and nieces and burning most of the letters, sending anything that she deemed too personal, or in any way discreditable to the Austen clan, up in smoke.

Survivors

LONGER LIVES
What happened to the other Austen family members? Most of them were notably long lived for their time. Even Jane's disabled brother George lived until he was 71. James was the exception, dying a couple of years after Jane.

Old Mrs Austen went on for another decade. Her grandson James Edward remembered her saying, 'I sometimes think that God Almighty must have forgotten me; but I dare say He will come for me in His own good time.' He did come, but only when she was 88 years old.

Edward dealt with his troubles and died rich as ever in 1852. Henry remarried – Eleanor Jackson, an old friend of the family – in 1820, moved to a curacy in Farnham, then briefly served as chaplain to the British Embassy in Berlin, and spent time in France before finally returning to Kent where he died in 1850; Frank made a surprise late marriage to Martha Lloyd, became Sir Francis Austen in 1837 and died in 1865. Charles was still serving abroad, in Burma, when he caught cholera and died in 1852.

Jane's Favourite Nieces

Anna Austen Lefroy's writing ambitions were dashed by raising her family of eight. 'Poor Animal, she will be worn out before she is thirty', Jane had written, presciently, in March 1817. After Ben Lefroy's death, she had some minor works published, and attempted, unsuccessfully, to finish *Sanditon*. She died in 1872, aged 79.

Fanny Knight married a much older baronet in 1820; Sir Edward Knatchbull already had six children, and they had nine more together. She died in 1882, aged 89. A letter written to Marianne, her younger sister, in 1869, rather spoils her image for Austen lovers:

'They [the Austen family] were not rich & the people around with whom they chiefly mixed, were not at all high bred... Aunt Jane was too clever not to put aside all possible signs of "common-ness"... & teach herself to be more refined... if it had not been for Papa's marriage which brought them into Kent... they [Cassandra and Jane] would have been, tho' not less clever & agreeable in themselves, very much below par as to good Society & its ways.'

Illness, Death and Legacy

The snobbishness of the recollection leaves a bad taste in the mouth; it also gives most of the credit for Jane's 'learned refinement' to Fanny's mother, Elizabeth. By the time it was written, though, Fanny Knatchbull was into her seventies, and a late Victorian, and these factors will have coloured her view of Jane, a countrywoman and a Georgian, then dead for over five decades.

Right and below: Sir Edward Knatchbull, who married Fanny Knight in 1820, and the Knatchbull family's seat, the beautiful Palladian Hatch House in Kent, designed by the architect Robert Adam.

Opposite page: Painted around 1845, Frank Austen depicted in his distinguished old age.

Out of Print

Slow Burn
Now that Austen's popularity has been stellar for well over a century and shows no sign of waning, it's surprising to look back on how slowly it grew. Her works were so far from being immediate classics that at one point they were out of print for over a decade.

The Collected Edition
After the 1831 idea for a collected works published by John Murray failed, a publisher called Richard Bentley approached Cassandra and Henry, who was still helping his sister in publishing matters, and asked if he could buy the copyrights for Jane's novels for £250. We don't know why they said yes to such a modest deal, but Jane's literary prominence had, if anything, shrunk over the previous few years, and Henry and Cassandra were neither of them young – perhaps it was just the easiest way to get her back into print. Bentley chiselled – when it became clear that he'd have to buy the rights to *Pride and Prejudice* separately, he took the £40 it cost off the total and paid £210 instead.

Finding a Likeness
Bentley wanted a portrait of the author for a frontispiece, but the family don't seem to have offered the picture that would later become the standard: a rough little half-length sketch by Cassandra, showing a slightly grumpy-looking seated Jane, arms firmly crossed. Bentley instead commissioned handsome illustrations, showing key scenes from the novels, for the books.

He was one of a new generation of publishers, determined to get books to a wider – and poorer – audience than previously. His books weren't cheap, but they weren't prohibitively expensive either; his collection of Austen would appear in a new series called Bentley's Standard Novels, each title in a single volume, apart from the shorter *Persuasion* and *Northanger Abbey*, which were twinned in one book.

A Fresh View

Henry updated his biographical note for the new series, making Jane sound rather more literary and a bit less of a domestic goddess. Among his additions was an anecdote about Jane's refusal to attend a soiree at which the celebrated French author Madame de Staël would be present. De Staël was famous – her 1807 novel *Corinne, or Italy* had outsold even the novels of Walter Scott – but not respectable. Henry's point was that his gently bred sister would not have wanted to meet her socially. (For her part, De Staël is reported to have considered *Pride and Prejudice* workaday and *vulgaire*.)

Bentley's collection didn't ignite Jane's fame in a big way, but it kept her in the public consciousness for the next couple of decades. He began with printings of a maximum of 3,000 for each title, adding smaller reprints as individual titles sold out.

Below: Madame de Staël, painted by Vladimir Borovikovsky in 1812, with the title page of the American translation of her smash hit novel *Corinne*. Rich, highly political and a noted philosopher, she moved in elevated social circles and was famous for her salons, as well as her liberated – scandalous – behaviour: altogether the antithesis of the Jane Austen whose modest image Henry sought to protect.

Opposite, left: Richard Bentley, the publisher who spotted a market for Austen's novels after they had gone out of print.

Opposite, right: Cassandra's original sketch of Jane – the only portrait that it's certain was painted during her lifetime, although family members felt it wasn't a good likeness.

Preserving Jane's Image

REMEMBERING AUNT JANE
By the 1860s, Jane Austen's own generation was gone. It was left to the battalion of nephews and nieces to produce the first real memoir of their aunt. As author, James Edward Austen-Leigh led the way, but the project was a joint effort with everyone who remembered Jane contributing their own stories.

Opposite top: The 'compromise' engraving, which everyone agreed didn't look like Austen. Nevertheless, it's been the default portrait of her ever since, even making it onto the Bank of England's £10 note – perhaps appropriately the first British bank note made of polymer – in 2017.

Opposite bottom: An 1898 Brock illustration depicting the socially climbing Mrs Elton, showing off her inappropriate finery to Emma Woodhouse.

The First Memoir

A Memoir of Jane Austen came out in 1869. The approach it took was quite similar to that of the first version of Henry's biographical notice, although it was much longer. It depicted Jane as naturally highly gifted, but also refined, pious and retiring. The novels were portrayed as genteel drawing-room romances with skilled and natural depictions of character.

What it left out was any mention of the harder, more satirical edge of Austen's writing: the rather limited subject of this biography could never have created Mr and Mrs Elton, or Mrs Norris.

James Edward would unintentionally have reinforced the views of romantics like Charlotte Brontë. Brontë had read *Pride and Prejudice* on the recommendation of the celebrated critic G. H. Lewes, but the virtues cited by the memoir seemed like limitations to Brontë – in 1848, she wrote that she found 'no glance of a bright vivid physiognomy… no fresh air – no blue hill… I should hardly like to live with her ladies and gentlemen in their elegant but confined houses… Miss Austen is only shrewd and observant.' It seems that she, too, missed the satire.

Even if it was bland, the memoir kickstarted a new enthusiasm for Austen – it attracted reviews in its own right and generated much more critical interest in her work. The last of her novels came out of copyright in 1860, too, so any publisher could now bring out their own editions.

Jane's New Look

When the memoir needed a portrait, Cassandra's rough sketch was sent to James Andrews of Maidenhead, to be used as the basis for a new watercolour. The result smoothed down the edges: the arms were uncrossed, the expression made more tranquil, the eyes larger and the cap more neatly pleated; it was the basis for the engraving that appeared on the frontispiece. The family felt it looked even less like Jane than the original, and it certainly has less character, but it has been used to depict her ever since.

'I think the portrait is very much superior to anything that could have been expected from the sketch… It is a very pleasing sweet face, tho', I confess, to not thinking it much like the original; but that, the public may not be able to detect.'

—Letter from Cassy, Charles Austen's daughter, not finding a likeness – but also noting that it doesn't matter much, 18 December 1869

Illness, Death and Legacy   151

JANE AUSTEN.

LONDON: RICHARD BENTLEY, 1870.

Conquering the World

FAVOURITE NOVELS
In 1869, Bentley brought out all six Austen titles as part of a new series, Favourite Novels, and this was followed in 1882 by a third collection, specific to Austen, called The Steventon Edition.

The Academic Angle

The focus on Jane as an innovator had begun, and her work would shortly come under a level of both critical analysis and popular appreciation that has hardly been given to any other author before or since.

The first scholarly edition of the novels was an annotated set published in 1923 by the Clarendon Press and edited by the Oxford academics R. W. Chapman and Katherine Metcalfe. Although the first edition of Jane's letters had been brought out by Fanny Knatchbull's son, Lord Braborne, in 1884 – consisting of the letters that Fanny had owned – in 1932 Chapman also brought out his expanded edited edition of Jane Austen's letters. Their everyday content attracted some criticism, but that they weren't consciously 'literary' has served both Austen fans and academics well ever since, because they give such a clear picture of her day-to-day life.

'Composition seems to me Impossible, with a head full of Joints of Mutton and doses of rhubarb.'

—Letter from Jane to Cassandra, complaining about life's commonplaces intruding on art, 8 September 1816

Austen was starting to find a place with readers at every level which has lasted ever since: you could buy a sixpenny copy of *Pride and Prejudice* for a quick romantic hit, or a handsome hardback for your home library, or, if you were of a more literary turn, an edition complete with all the scholarly apparatus.

Austen in Translation

Jane may never have been abroad, but her novels travelled early and extensively and can now be found all over the world. She was popular in translation from (almost) the first moment of publication, despite the challenge to translators posed by her very individual combination of plain language and subtle inference. Heavily abridged versions of *Pride and Prejudice* (*Les Cinq Filles de Monsieur Bennet*) and *Mansfield Park* appeared in French partworks in 1813 and 1815 respectively, and all her works had been translated into French by 1824. Germany and Portugal were also early adopters, although at first translating just one or two titles rather than all six.

In Germany she was published in the well-regarded Tauchnitz series of novels in translation from 1864, and regularly reprinted. Some of the earlier translations take surprising liberties: one French translation of *Sense and Sensibility* has a repentant Willoughby marry the woman he seduced and abandoned. And some countries were much slower adopters than others: the first Dutch translation only appeared in 1922, and Austen only made it to Moscow in the late 1960s.

Below: Two of the early French translations of Austen – *Les Cinq Filles de M. Bennet*, and *Persuasion*, published as *La Famille Elliot* in 1821.

Opposite page: A political cartoon of Lord Braborne, a Liberal politician, published in 1870; in a more literary role, he was the first to publish, in 1884, those of Austen's letters that had been sent to his mother, Fanny Knatchbull.

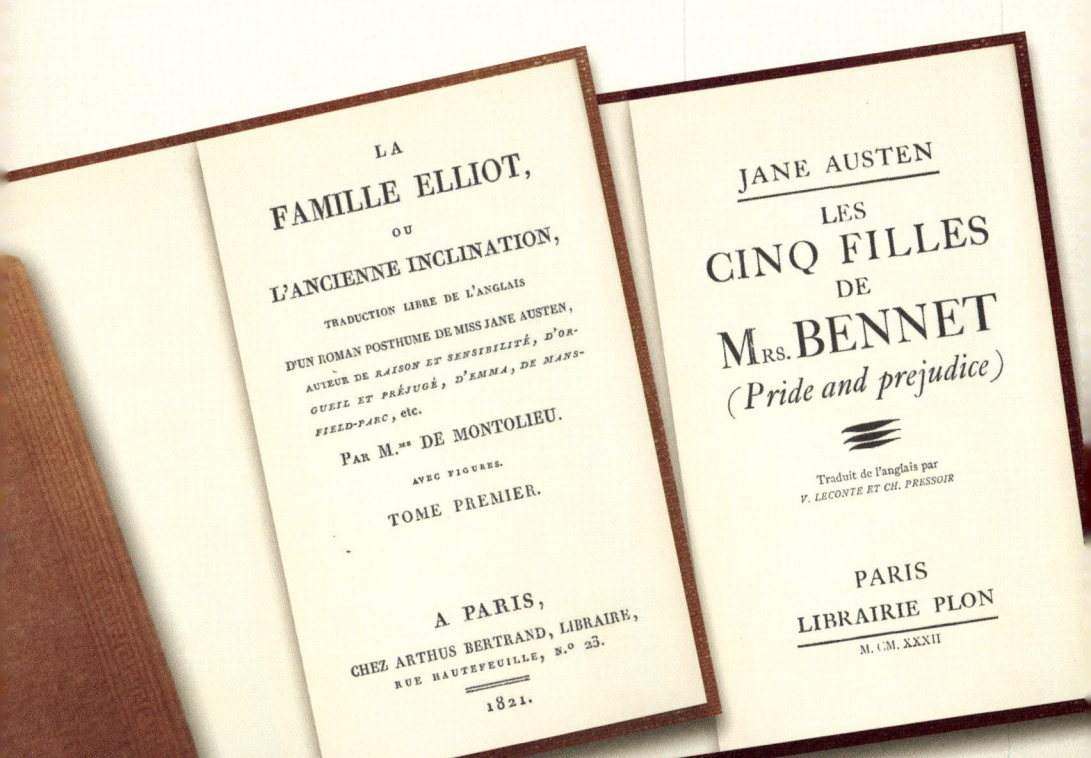

Catching Her in Greatness

ENDURING POPULARITY
Austen mania may have started slowly, but in the first quarter of the 21st century, Jane's novels have become unassailable: a constant supply of films ensures that she's available to those who prefer to watch their books; there is an ever-increasing library of criticism devoted to every aspect of her work, and she's maintained her original standing as an author of popular romances.

Different Austens

Which Austen a reader finds when they pick up a book depends on them: far from being limited, her work is endlessly flexible, surely the key to the breadth of its appeal. In the 1920s, Virginia Woolf found that she was the hardest author to catch in the act – that even close word-by-word analysis of her writing doesn't yield up the secret that makes her so different from other writers.

By 1939, D. W. Harding, a lecturer in psychology, was finding that Jane Austen, far from being kind and genteel, used writing as a vehicle for 'regulated hatred' – her satire becoming a safety valve for observations about the nastier aspects of everyday society.

Anybody who has had the temerity to write about Jane Austen is aware of two facts: First, that of all great writers she is the most difficult to catch in the act of greatness; second, that there are 25 elderly gentlemen living in the neighborhood of London who resent any slight upon her genius as if it were an insult offered to the chastity of their aunts.'

—Virginia Woolf, reviewing Chapman's edition of Austen – and noting that some fans already felt that 'the divine Jane' was beyond criticism, 1924

Illness, Death and Legacy

Today, her every word has been examined, from every imaginable aspect: what her novels tell us about the different levels of society, or the slave trade, or land ownership, or the state of Anglicanism in the 19th century, or the Napoleonic Wars, have all been analysed and discussed, and there are still many more readers who read her books, without further analysis, for pleasure. Benjamin Disraeli, Prime Minister and a novelist himself, a busy man, once asked if he had time to *read* any of her novels, is said to have replied 'Yes, all six. Every year.' But for the first-time (or the tenth-time) reader, she still offers an immediate satisfaction – that of carefully composed plots neatly executed, with characters that are immaculately drawn without – in the main – there being any awkward joins, and, underlying it all a constant stream of common sense.

Below left: Benjamin Disraeli, who allegedly found time to read all six Austen novels annually.

Below: The beautifully bound, Thomson-illustrated George Allen edition of *Pride and Prejudice* produced in 1894.

Opposite page: Virginia Woolf, one of the first truly modern critics of Austen.

Bibliography and References

In Print

Adkins, Lesley & Roy, *Eavesdropping on Jane Austen's England*, Abacus, 2014

Austen, Jane, *Teenage Writings*, Oxford University Press, 2017

Austen-Leigh, James Edward, *A Memoir of Jane Austen, and Other Family Recollections*, Oxford University Press, 2008

Barchas, Janine, *Matters of Fact in Jane Austen: History, Location, and Celebrity*, Johns Hopkins University Press, 2013

Byrne, Paula, *The Real Jane Austen: A Life in Small Things*, William Collins, 2014

Clery, E. J., *Jane Austen: The Banker's Sister*, Biteback Publishing, 2017

Davidson, Hilary, *Jane Austen's Wardrobe*, Yale University Press, 2023

Gehrer, Julienne, *Martha Lloyd's Household Book*, Bodleian Library, 2021

Harman, Claire, *Jane's Fame*, Canongate Books, 2010

Kelly, Helena, *Jane Austen: The Secret Radical*, Icon Books, 2016

Keymer, Tom, *Jane Austen: Writing, Society, Politics*, Oxford University Press, 2020

Le Faye, Deirdre (editor), *Jane Austen's Letters*, Oxford University Press, 2014

Le Faye, Deirdre, *Jane Austen: A Family Record*, Cambridge University Press, 2003

Le Faye, Deirdre, *Jane Austen: The World of Her Novels*, Frances Lincoln, 2003

Looser, Devoney, *The Making of Jane Austen*, Johns Hopkins University Press, 2017

Muir, Rory, *Love and Marriage in the Age of Jane Austen*, Yale University Press, 2024

Richetti, John (editor), *The Cambridge Companion to the Eighteenth-Century Novel*, Cambridge University Press, 2006

Tomalin, Claire, *Jane Austen: A Life*, Penguin, 2012

Walton, Geri, *Jane Austen's Cousin: The Outlandish Countess de Feuillide*, Pen & Sword Books, 2021

Worsley, Lucy, *Jane Austen at Home*, Hodder, 2018

Online

A vast number of online sources deal with every aspect of Austen and her times – from love and marriage to politics and daily life. Three of the most varied and comprehensive are:

All Things Jane Austen
allthingsjaneausten.net

The Jane Austen Society of North America
jasna.org
An online subscription journal, but with a number of articles that are free to read.

Jane Austen's World
janeaustensworld.com

Timeline of Jane Austen's Works

- **1775** Jane Austen is born on 16 December

- **ca. 1787–93** Writes the short works collectively known as the Juvenilia

- **ca. 1794** Begins writing *Lady Susan*

- **1795** Writes 'Elinor and Marianne' (*Sense and Sensibility*)

- **1796–97** Writes 'First Impressions' (*Pride and Prejudice*)

- **1798–99** Writes 'Susan' (*Northanger Abbey*)

- **1804** Begins writing *The Watsons* but does not complete it

- **1805** Finishes writing *Lady Susan*

- **1811** Publishes *Sense and Sensibility*; revises manuscript of *Pride and Prejudice*; begins writing *Mansfield Park*

- **1813** Publishes *Pride and Prejudice*

- **1814** Publishes *Mansfield Park*; begins writing *Emma*

- **1815** Publishes *Emma*; begins writing *Persuasion*

- **1816** Finishes writing *Persuasion*

- **1817** Begins writing *Sanditon*; Jane Austen dies on 18 July; *Northanger Abbey* and *Persuasion* published with 'Biographical Notice' by Henry Austen

- **1871** *Lady Susan* and fragment of *The Watsons* published in second edition of James Edward Austen-Leigh's *A Memoir of Jane Austen*

- **1925** Incomplete manuscript of *Sanditon* published

Index

academic reputation 152
adaptations 6, 154
alphabet blocks 38
Andrews, James 150
anti-heroines 42–3
army 46–7
art exhibitions 115
assemblies 48
Aunt Jane 98–9, 150
Austen, Anna (niece)
　99, 118–19, 137, 146
Austen, Caroline (niece)
　138–9
Austen, Cassandra (mother)
　10, 12–13, 15, 16, 19, 21, 49,
　84, 88–9, 134, 146
Austen, Cassandra (sister)
　15, 24–5, 26, 40, 44,
　62–3, 88–9, 98, 140–1,
　142, 144–5
　artworks 34, 148, 150
　engagement 48, 58–9
Austen, Charles (brother)
　15, 19, 47, 80, 146
Austen Knight, Edward
　(brother) 15, 19, 46,
　80, 85, 86, 117, 146
　adoption by the Knight
　family 27
Austen, Francis (brother)
　15, 19, 47, 80–1, 146
Austen, George (brother)
　14–15, 46, 146
Austen, George (father)
　10–11, 12–13, 14, 16,
　19, 21, 22, 24, 60, 68,
　77, 78–9
Austen, Henry (brother)
　15, 19, 29, 47, 80, 114, 122
　acting as literary agent
　74, 100, 120–1
　Biographical Note
　142–3, 146
Austen, James (brother)
　14–15, 30, 41, 46, 80, 146

Austen-Leigh, James
　Edward (nephew)
　18, 42, 76, 90, 146, 150
Baillie, Matthew, Dr 122
Bath 22, 64–7, 77, 80
　water cures 66
Beautifull Cassandra, The 35
Bentley, Richard 148–9
Bigg-Wither, Harris 70
book binding 109, 122
book subscriptions 22, 108–9
Brontë, Charlotte 7, 150
Brunton, Mary 93
Burney, Fanny
　22, 43, 53, 60, 108
Byron, Lord
　103, 111, 114, 120, 142

Cadell & Davies 60–1
Centlivre, Susanna 30
Chapman, R.W. 152, 154
Charlotte, Princess 103
Chawton Cottage
　41, 81, 86–7, 88,
　90, 117, 144
Chawton House
　89, 94, 117
church and clergy
　10–11, 16, 19, 20, 46–7, 125
Clarke, James Stanier 122–3
collected works 148–9
copyright 74, 104, 108–9, 113,
　120–1, 144, 148, 150
Cowper, William 23, 36

dancing 36, 40, 44, 48
Deane parsonage 11, 16, 64
dedications of works
　34–5, 123
De Feuillide, Eliza (cousin)
　19, 22, 28–9, 31, 35,
　43, 47, 104–5
de Staël, Madame 92, 149
Disraeli, Benjamin 155
Dutch editions 153

East India Company 28
Edgeworth, Maria 92
education 24–5, 26–7
Egerton, Thomas
　100, 103, 104, 108, 110, 120
Elinor and Marianne
　see *Sense and Sensibility*
Emma
　12, 17, 20, 26–7, 42, 49, 96–7
　writing 91, 118–19
　publication 120–1, 123
epistolary novels
　35, 43, 53

fashion 72–3
Fielding, Henry 23, 30, 53
First Impressions
　see *Pride and Prejudice*
Fowle, Tom 25, 48, 58–9
French editions 153
French Revolution 19, 29

George, Prince Regent
　103, 122–3
German editions 153
Godmersham 46, 85, 94
Gothic novels 35, 61, 74
gravestone inscription 141

Hancock, Philadelphia
　(aunt) 10, 15, 19, 28–9
Hancock, Tysoe Saul 28–9
Harding, D.W. 154
Hastings, Warren 28–9
holiday affair (rumoured) 69

illness
　134–5, 138–9, 140–1
India 19, 28–9
ink 38

Jane Austen House
　Museum 88
Johnson, Dr 23
juvenilia 30, 31, 34–5, 145

Timeline of Jane Austen's Works

- **1775** Jane Austen is born on 16 December

- **ca. 1787–93** Writes the short works collectively known as the Juvenilia

- **ca. 1794** Begins writing *Lady Susan*

- **1795** Writes 'Elinor and Marianne' (*Sense and Sensibility*)

- **1796–97** Writes 'First Impressions' (*Pride and Prejudice*)

- **1798–99** Writes 'Susan' (*Northanger Abbey*)

- **1804** Begins writing *The Watsons* but does not complete it

- **1805** Finishes writing *Lady Susan*

- **1811** Publishes *Sense and Sensibility*; revises manuscript of *Pride and Prejudice*; begins writing *Mansfield Park*

- **1813** Publishes *Pride and Prejudice*

- **1814** Publishes *Mansfield Park*; begins writing *Emma*

- **1815** Publishes *Emma*; begins writing *Persuasion*

- **1816** Finishes writing *Persuasion*

- **1817** Begins writing *Sanditon*; Jane Austen dies on 18 July; *Northanger Abbey* and *Persuasion* published with 'Biographical Notice' by Henry Austen

- **1871** *Lady Susan* and fragment of *The Watsons* published in second edition of James Edward Austen-Leigh's *A Memoir of Jane Austen*

- **1925** Incomplete manuscript of *Sanditon* published

Index

academic reputation 152
adaptations 6, 154
alphabet blocks 38
Andrews, James 150
anti-heroines 42–3
army 46–7
art exhibitions 115
assemblies 48
Aunt Jane 98–9, 150
Austen, Anna (niece)
    99, 118–19, 137, 146
Austen, Caroline (niece)
    138–9
Austen, Cassandra (mother)
    10, 12–13, 15, 16, 19, 21, 49,
    84, 88–9, 134, 146
Austen, Cassandra (sister)
    15, 24–5, 26, 40, 44,
    62–3, 88–9, 98, 140–1,
    142, 144–5
    artworks 34, 148, 150
    engagement 48, 58–9
Austen, Charles (brother)
    15, 19, 47, 80, 146
Austen Knight, Edward
    (brother) 15, 19, 46,
    80, 85, 86, 117, 146
    adoption by the Knight
    family 27
Austen, Francis (brother)
    15, 19, 47, 80–1, 146
Austen, George (brother)
    14–15, 46, 146
Austen, George (father)
    10–11, 12–13, 14, 16,
    19, 21, 22, 24, 60, 68,
    77, 78–9
Austen, Henry (brother)
    15, 19, 29, 47, 80, 114, 122
    acting as literary agent
    74, 100, 120–1
    Biographical Note
    142–3, 146
Austen, James (brother)
    14–15, 30, 41, 46, 80, 146

Austen-Leigh, James
    Edward (nephew)
    18, 42, 76, 90, 146, 150
Baillie, Matthew, Dr 122
Bath 22, 64–7, 77, 80
    water cures 66
Beautifull Cassandra, The 35
Bentley, Richard 148–9
Bigg-Wither, Harris 70
book binding 109, 122
book subscriptions 22, 108–9
Brontë, Charlotte 7, 150
Brunton, Mary 93
Burney, Fanny
    22, 43, 53, 60, 108
Byron, Lord
    103, 111, 114, 120, 142

Cadell & Davies 60–1
Centlivre, Susanna 30
Chapman, R.W. 152, 154
Charlotte, Princess 103
Chawton Cottage
    41, 81, 86–7, 88,
    90, 117, 144
Chawton House
    89, 94, 117
church and clergy
    10–11, 16, 19, 20, 46–7, 125
Clarke, James Stanier 122–3
collected works 148–9
copyright 74, 104, 108–9, 113,
    120–1, 144, 148, 150
Cowper, William 23, 36

dancing 36, 40, 44, 48
Deane parsonage 11, 16, 64
dedications of works
    34–5, 123
De Feuillide, Eliza (cousin)
    19, 22, 28–9, 31, 35,
    43, 47, 104–5
de Staël, Madame 92, 149
Disraeli, Benjamin 155
Dutch editions 153

East India Company 28
Edgeworth, Maria 92
education 24–5, 26–7
Egerton, Thomas
    100, 103, 104, 108, 110, 120
Elinor and Marianne
    see *Sense and Sensibility*
Emma
    12, 17, 20, 26–7, 42, 49, 96–7
    writing 91, 118–19
    publication 120–1, 123
epistolary novels
    35, 43, 53

fashion 72–3
Fielding, Henry 23, 30, 53
First Impressions
    see *Pride and Prejudice*
Fowle, Tom 25, 48, 58–9
French editions 153
French Revolution 19, 29

George, Prince Regent
    103, 122–3
German editions 153
Godmersham 46, 85, 94
Gothic novels 35, 61, 74
gravestone inscription 141

Hancock, Philadelphia
    (aunt) 10, 15, 19, 28–9
Hancock, Tysoe Saul 28–9
Harding, D.W. 154
Hastings, Warren 28–9
holiday affair (rumoured) 69

illness
    134–5, 138–9, 140–1
India 19, 28–9
ink 38

Jane Austen House
    Museum 88
Johnson, Dr 23
juvenilia 30, 31, 34–5, 145

Kean, Edmund 114–15
Knight, Fanny (niece)
99, 118–19, 134–5,
139, 146, 152

Lady Susan 42–3
La Fontaine, Jean de 22
landscapes 96–7
La Tournelle, Mrs 26
Lefroy, Madam
44, 50–1, 63
Lefroy, Tom 44, 51, 63
legal disputes 84–5, 117, 127
Leigh-Perrot, James (uncle)
48, 65, 66, 84–5, 124
letters 7, 44–5, 62–3, 152
libraries 22, 50, 65, 92
Lloyd, Martha
38, 41, 49, 80–1, 87, 88–9, 146
London 114–15
love, writing about 54–5
Love and Freindship 35
Lovers' Vows 31
Lyme Regis 68, 77

Mansfield Park
12, 19, 29, 31, 36, 47, 95
writing 91
publication 112–13
Manydown 41, 70, 94
marriage market 48
marriage proposal 70–1
Memoir of Jane Austen, A
42, 92, 150
militia 6–7
Miss Catherine
see *Northanger Abbey*
Murray, John
120–1, 128–9, 142, 144
music 36

Napoleonic Wars
124, 130, 155
navy 19, 46–7, 131
Northanger Abbey
12, 23, 35, 67
writing 63, 91
publication 74–5, 142
novel reading 23, 92–3

Oxford 10–11, 13, 26, 46

paper 38–9
parsonage life 20–1
Persuasion
12, 19, 47, 67, 73, 96
writing
91, 129, 130–1, 135
publication 142
poetry 23, 36, 51, 87
portraits of Jane Austen
148, 150
posthumous publications
42, 74, 76, 129, 136–7,
142–5, 148–53
posthumous reputation
148–55
Pride and Prejudice
12, 17, 20, 39, 55, 73, 94
writing 53, 91, 103
publication
60, 104–5, 108, 110–11
printing process
101, 109, 128
publishing anonymously
101, 105, 116
publishing deals
60–1, 74–5, 100, 108–9,
113, 120–1, 144

Quarterly Review, The
120, 128
Quentin, Harriet 115
quill pens 38–9

Radcliffe, Ann 61
reading 22–3, 36–7, 38
reviews
110–11, 126–7,
128–9, 143
Richardson, Samuel 23
Russian editions 153

Sanditon 136–7, 146
schools 24–5, 26–7
Scott, Walter 128–9
sea bathing 68–9
seaside resorts
68–9, 136

Sense and Sensibility
12, 20, 36, 54, 73
writing 52–3, 91, 129
publication
100–1, 102–3, 108
servants 21, 88
Shakespeare 36, 115
Sharp, Anne 94, 102, 138
Sheridan, Richard Brinsley
30, 111
Smith, Charlotte 23, 61
Southampton
22, 26, 81, 86
Sterne, Laurence 23
Steventon parsonage
11, 14, 16, 20–1, 24,
30, 41, 52–3, 64
Stoneleigh Abbey 84–5, 94
Susan
see *Northanger Abbey*

theatre 30–1, 114–15
timeline of works 157
translated editions 153

Victorian representation
6, 18, 62, 147

Watsons, The 76–7
West Indies 19, 58, 136
Weymouth 69
Winchester 140–1
Woolf, Virginia 7, 155
writing equipment 38–9
lap desk 52
writing process
38–9, 90–1
manuscripts
76, 92, 136
revisions
52, 74, 92, 100, 129

Credits

The publisher would like to thank the following for permission to reproduce copyright material. All reasonable efforts have been made to trace copyright holders and to obtain their permission for the use of copyright material. The publisher apologizes for any errors or omissions and will gratefully incorporate any corrections in future reprints if notified.

Alamy: 6 right; 7 right & left; 11; 23; 37; 40; 47 top; 53 bottom; 72 right; 118, 138; 145; 147 bottom; 148 right

Bath In Time: 79

Bibliothèques de Nancy: 22 right

Bridgeman Images: 35; 44; 46; 51; 86; 123 bottom, 125

Creative Commons: 12; 16 left, Collection of Auckland Museum Tamaki Paenga Hira; 17, British Library; 18 left, Sothebys; 19 left & right; 22 left; 26 & 27, Yale Center for British Art; 28, Gemäldegalerie der Staatlichen Museen zu Berlin; 29, Yale Center for British Art; 30, British Museum; 31, University of Illinois Urbana-Champaign University Library; 38, National Library of Australia; 39, George Allen; 41; 42, The Morgan Library; 43; 45, National Library of Australia; 47 bottom, Charles M. Lefferts; 48, Houghton Library; 49 left & right; 50 right, British Library; 52, Harold B. Lee Library; 54 right & 55 left, British Library; 55 right; 60–61; 65 left; 66, Metropolitan Museum of Art; 67, Yale Center for British Art; 71, Lily Library Indiana University; 76 right, Sothebys; 81 top, Nicholas Pocock; 84, British Museum; 87; 88, R ferroni2000; 93; 94 & 95 bottom British Library; 95 top, Flickr; 96–97, Yale Center for British Art; 97 bottom, Lily Library Indiana University; 98; 101 British Library; 102; 103 top, Yale Center for British Art; 103 bottom, Royal Collection; 104 left, British Library; 105 left, Lily Library Indiana University; 105 right, British Library; 108, The Repository of arts, literature, commerce, manufactures, fashions and politics (1809); 109 right, Library Company of Philadelphia; 110, British Library; 111 left, Hermitage Museum; 111 right, National Portrait Gallery; 112, British Library; 113, University of California Libraries; 115 left, British Museum; 115 right, Los Angeles County Museum of Art; 119, British Library; 121 left, National Portrait Gallery; 123 top, Victoria and Albert Museum; 128; 129, National Galleries Scotland; 131; 137, FIT; 141, Lily Library Indiana University; 142, Lily Library Indiana University; 144; 146; 147 top, Art Value; 148 left, Library of Congress; 149 left, Tretyakov Gallery; 151 left; 153 left & right; 154; 155 left, National Portrait Gallery; 155 centre, National Library NZ; 155 right, British Library

Danmarks Nationalleksikon: 53 top

Dreamstime: 80

Getty Images: 14; 24 left; 54 left; 62 left; 77; 90; 100; 120 left; 121 right; 126; 134; 136; 140; 143

Internet Archive: 13, 50, left; 63, 74–75; 76 left

Library of Congress: 18 right; 24 right; 58; 64; 149 right

Look And Learn History Picture Archive: 10, Wellcome Collection; 16 right, Cleveland Museum of Art; 20, Yale Center for British Art; 36; 68–69, New York Public Library; 114 left, Metropolitan Museum of Art; 114 right, New York Public Library; 122 right, Birmingham Museums Trust; 152, Yale Center for British Art

National Gallery of Art: 62 right

Picryl: 59

Raw Pixel: 97 top; 109 left, 116; 124; 127

Shutterstock: 130; 151 right

Store Norske Leksikon: 92

Tessa Digital Collections of the Los Angeles Public Library: 73

Wellcome Collection: 78, 139